Scarred Butterfly

J.M. Duell

WEBSITES

http://ParanormalPerspective.net

http://jemduell.wordpress.com

http://instagram.com/lonelyspiritguiding

http://twitter.com/ParaAuthorJ

http://allpoetry.com/White_Phantom

http://national-paranormal-society.org/author/jen/

ARTICLES

AUTHOR - N.P.S. FOCUS (AN ONLINE MAGAZINE)

Scarred Butterfly

ISBN-13: 978-1535454841

ISBN-10: 1535454849

To my mother who never gave up,
and never allowed me to, either.

We survived!

Contents:

Preface

In the early fall of 2010 as I worked diligently on my creative works; a voice from within kept insisting that I put my own story down on paper. This concept completely frightened me and yet it provoked me to inherit the truth as it were. I was completely trapped in an unwanted relationship without any idea of how to escape. If ever he'd suspect that I was about to get out, those ever so famous words would pass his lips; "If you ever leave me, I will kill you and whoever is with you." Ah, yes, control. The narcissist's best friend.

His false emotions and temporary lulls were sometimes nice, but they were few and far between. I did the unthinkable; I denied myself by pretending that I couldn't see the truth. By living in denial of what was before me, I was able to adapt temporary peace coupled with handfuls of discomfort. My reveries were silently suffering as well - only fields of grayscale and lugubrious scenes danced around like funeral friends coming by to say "hello" - but I wouldn't be deterred from the grander scheme of life as I was convinced that a whole world was out there waiting for me to enter it.

As I spent time in public, I quietly observed the happier couples. Their smiles gleamed in a playful romance; I'd wonder what it would feel like to know a love like that. The sort of love that resonates truly from the heart and not the fist. The type of love that complements instead of insults. The style of love that caresses and appreciates instead of absurd accusations and discouragement. Reality soon crept in and tore me from the wonder and thus my eyes focused on my surroundings. What a darkened veil of deceit I was caught in ...

I grew tired of simply dreaming and silently crying.

With a sudden and unexpected situation and no time to think; I made a life-changing decision that unlocked that prison door forever. I boldly stepped out into the waiting world with nothing but a checkered box full of charcoal illustration pencils and the clothes on my back. Facing that vast unknown was the hardest thing that I had ever had to do but it was also the best decision I've ever made.

In my recovery I have discovered a lot about myself to include accepting that it wasn't my fault. It's too easy to blame ourselves and consider that we must be doing something wrong and somehow deserve the abuse. If we assign ourselves the sentence of wrongful acceptance then we are literally handing them a power over us that they do not deserve. We are individuals and we do not ask for the torture that comes from abuse. If I can teach you anything from my situation then I have succeeded in helping you see that you do not deserve to suffer. It is human to make some mistakes and I want you to know that it is okay. It is not okay for someone to hurt you or cut you down, nobody is perfect and accidents happen.

Because I know that a lot of you may feel trapped, I took on the challenge of telling my story as a way to help you to see that you deserve better. I'm praying that as you flip through these pages, you can relate to me and see that it is time to choose your own path. There are so many men and women out there who lived through these types of abusive relationships who are either still there, or stronger for leaving.

Your partner is supposed to stand by you and love you for who you are. They accept your faults as you accept theirs. Falling in love shouldn't hurt, it should be wonderful and filled with bliss. I write this from experience; I now have the kind of love that makes me feel amazing and special. To wake up knowing that the other person is happy to be with me is a dream come true. I used to believe that I would never experience real love but the truth is that it's out there for all of us. The difference from my former relationship to my current one is like night and day. My only regret is that I didn't realize it much sooner and yet I consider that I felt as though I was wandering hell completely alone.

... I was not alone! There are so many people who have lived through abusive relationships who found the courage to finally escape. There are too many who are either too afraid or unaware of how to get out.

The day before Easter I decided to get my hair styled with my youngest daughter. As the woman sat me down and prepped me, she had asked me what it was I do for a living. I proceeded to explain to her that I was an author and I am currently working on an autobiography of how I survived two decades of abuse. She stopped for a moment, and then looked at me and said "Good for you, I survived 16 years myself." Her story was rather similar to mine; the only difference was that she was able to access articles by other abuse survivors which empowered her to get free. I hope I can do the same for someone out there who will pick up my book and read it. My goal is to help and empower as many people as I can reach by telling my story.

If I can do it after two decades, then so can you. There is hope out there and it's a beautiful world just waiting for you to step out and close that door on the abuse.

Chapter 1

battered woman syndrome n.

The highly variable symptom complex of physical and psychological injuries exhibited by a woman repeatedly abused especially physically by her mate — called also battered woman's syndrome, battered wife syndrome, battered women's syndrome.

~ merriam-webster.com - medical dictionary

My earliest memories of life were both happy and sad. The scents of blooming gardens and freshwater lakes race me back to a time where I truly believed that life was magical and filled with unlimited opportunity. I had a deep passion for sports and nature - with that came aspiring dreams of one day playing basketball on the

Syracuse University women's team. With nature; there wasn't a day I can recall of being inside long enough to sit through an entire half-hour program on television. I recognized that I had this enormous imagination in which I'd remain outdoors and run through the fields and forests behind the house until it was time for dinner. Many afternoons were spent with my younger brother and friends out behind our North Chittenango home catching bullfrogs and tadpoles.

The one memory which has always stayed with me happened when I was 5 years old; I wandered alone in this enormous field while wearing a pure white cotton dress complete with dark stockings and black clogs. I was walking through a thick patch of overgrown weeds and dandelions trying to keep up with a rabbit I'd been chasing. A group of monarch butterflies and dragonflies seemed to follow me up to a point where I reached a large oak tree in the center of this field. The rabbit stopped at the base of this tree and looked at me. I stood still while looking back at him and recognized that at that moment, I was extremely happy. I felt like nature had accepted me into a realm that most people never experience (or never care to) and I just observed the butterflies, the dragonflies and the rabbit. Before long, the sky darkened and thunderclaps disturbed the calm afternoon. The rabbit turned and continued on its way as did the butterflies and dragonflies which left me to tread back through the thick weeds towards the house alone. I wasn't scared nor concerned but sad that I had to leave this place of tranquility due to a darkening storm approaching - a theme that would later permeate my life.

Freedom wasn't something that ever crossed my mind between the duties of being successful in school and the normal home chores of dishes and vacuuming. My childhood was by no means perfect; we had our own share of downs as a family - my father in his younger years was quite hard on my brother, and my parents had fought quite often. Most of us can honestly say that our parents weren't perfect people and most of us probably can share a memory which is a bit more displeasing than the happier ones filled with birthday wishes coming true and pleasantly playful afternoons.

The disagreements between my parents stemmed from bouts of alcoholism and frustrations of keeping a family together and functional. In no way today do I hold anything against either parent, nor do I blame them for a single thing in my life. Rather, I am proud to have them in my life and appreciate their ongoing support.

It was obvious to both my brother and I that our parents would eventually get a divorce. The realization of the split-up didn't come into full-bloom until I was about 13 years old. I remember feeling a sense of blame, and a lot of confusion about what was unfolding and tried to keep my brother calm (who had taken the news of the separation a bit harder than I had.) My mother had a secret, but my father did as well. Both secrets were quite impressionable on both my brother and I; in that phase of life (pre-teen to teenager) we are already confused and troubled - anything added to that can really send you on a downward spiral rather quickly if you aren't careful.

My father's secret wasn't *too* secret at all, but rather something we rarely spoke of outside of our home. He was struggling with the effects of anxiety, dyslexia and obsessive compulsive disorder. Though I mentioned earlier that most of my childhood seemed inarguably happy, there are also some memories that I think back to today which bring tears to my eyes.

For a brief period of time, our family lived in a rented house on Oneida lake in the very small town of Lakeport. That house as I remember it wasn't too big nor too fancy but it was enough for a young growing family such as ours. Both of my parents at this point were working - my mother at the P&C supermarket in the village of Chittenango (now known as Tops Supermarkets) and my father at the Carrier Transicold factory in East Syracuse.

One afternoon while my mother was away at work, my brother and I were home with our father. As a child, I had an incredible amount of energy and exhibited a lot of restlessness. There was no slowing me down, I had a very active imagination and sought out ways to act it out. My brother kind of followed everything I started so if I was throwing toys around, he'd join me in this and before long, it was a pretty loud and noisy situation while during play time.

My father was just about at his wits end with me at some point one specific afternoon and came out of his bedroom with a shotgun and he held it up to my face and he said "I am sick of you kids." (keep in mind I was just 4 years old going on 5)

I stared back at him, and the gun and I had absolutely no idea at that time the severity of what was going on. In fact, I don't remember much beyond that moment, though I do remember that a series of concerning activity would continue up through to my teenage years.

It came in handfuls of name-calling and insults for things that were small in nature and rather mundane. Through these on and off sessions of abuse; our mother would try to protect us and situations would sometimes get out of control. It would develop into fists flying and items being thrown across the room. Luckily, we didn't witness most of the fights as she would send us upstairs before they'd begin. But if the abuse wasn't enough, the curse of excessive drinking followed.

In a way to cope with the ongoing struggle within our home, my mother had turned to alcohol as a way to cope. There were many nights that we were left alone in the house while she was away someplace drinking. I used to believe that it was normal - she would be gone for hours and we would be upstairs playing or in the kitchen going through cupboards.

She had her secrets as well. Not only was she trying to protect us from a possible explosion from our father, but she was discovering herself and acknowledging that she was homosexual. When I think about the things that she had to juggle, I can honestly say that I can't personally imagine how painful the struggle within these things had to have been for my mother. I imagine this weighed heavily on the marriage and would explain why my father had some of the outbursts of anger I had witnessed. Today, I hold no anger towards either parent, but recognize that they just weren't meant to be together.

Despite the arguments and the nights my brother and I were left alone in the house, I think they did the best they could given the circumstances they were living under. Eventually the divorce came. It really upset me that my parents were separating, but even in my 13 year old brain, I knew it was for the best. The emotions that I experienced during the divorce were both painful and equally confusing. I loved both of them, and I didn't want to choose a side. I supported my mother and saw the immeasurable pain in which she endured. I loved my father, but he was better at hiding some of the things he was going through. In no way did I want to be caught in the middle; I recited having fear for my father to the family court judge and it was decided that we'd only get 2 hours of visitation with him on every Sunday.

Was I really fearful? A part of me, not really. The other part knew however that he loved me and I shouldn't feel afraid, at least not as much as I made out to the judge. Perhaps I have an amount of regret for that today, but it is something I can't undo. I can however tell you that this taught me some much needed lessons I'd have to rediscover later in life.

As my mom now came into full bloom with who she was, she also found strength within herself to face those alcohol demons and kick the disease in the ass. I am proud to write that I watched her overcome alcoholism and she did it with the assistance of the 'Alcoholics Anonymous' program (otherwise known as A.A.) As she came into her own, I had to now come to terms with accepting my mother as gay, and this actually came easy for me. I saw immediate changes within her that were quite inspiring. She was happier, free, unafraid to be who she was, strong, and unknowingly my role model. I had watched her leave a bad marriage, kick a serious alcohol addiction, and all the while remain able to care for my brother and I. At some point, we even took my aunt in and my mother helped her out in a time where she really needed it. To say the least, my mother conquered the highest mountains and the most painful situations and came out of it gracefully; that alone deserves the highest praise possible.

Not only was my childhood nothing to marvel over; I also endured some real rough times through my school years. I had always been a little different than the other kids. I have this real vivid imagination which inspired me to go beyond the latest trends or be a member of some cliquish gathering. As well, I had dreams that took me well beyond the walls and rumor mills that thrive in the teenage world. I was deeply artistic and unafraid to show it, and for that I suffered at the hands of many insecure and cruel bullies.

From elementary school straight up to high school, I just didn't belong to any social group, nor did they want me to. I had a specific love for the creative arts and music, and most of my focus went there which left the rest of it on athletics.

I guess one could say that I was very socially awkward. I would go from periods of loneliness to sporadic moments of desperation and back to brief snippets of profound sadness. Some days, I was lucky enough to catch a break and was able to exist without crying or sitting with a flood of depressing thoughts washing over me. I really began to suffer a real deep level of clinical depression that I couldn't readily overcome. The thoughts of being useless and meaningless often surfaced in the back of my mind, and it was rather hard for me to focus on anything else - I couldn't understand at that time why these kids were so cruel to me, nor could I even begin to relate for that matter. What I did understand was that despite my desire to have productive friendships, I just wasn't able to be successful at it. A struggle that would continue into my adult life.

The effects of how I was being treated from peers in school ultimately overcame me at a pace that couldn't be slowed down nor controlled. When you begin to lose a sense of peace within, you also begin to lose yourself.

It wasn't long before I crossed peers who were drinking and smoking. I had nowhere else to turn; I found a temporary comfort within the use of alcohol and even marijuana. I wanted to reach out to my mother, but I really didn't believe at the time that she'd understand or that she'd be able to help me. Tension started growing within our house and because I was in so much turmoil, I ventured away from reaching out, and wandered towards a spiral of bad decisions.

Being in the *wrong* crowd is easy for a depressed teenager. I also had some rights; just before I spiraled downward, my mother had placed me into martial arts courses. The practices and training were very positive for me but like school, I found it hard to truly belong. There was a fear deep within which had manifested that prevented me from even trying. My focus was also lost to obsessive thoughts in which I struggled to handle. Those thoughts ranged from running away to drinking away those damning feelings of hurting myself to intoxicating thoughts of suicide. I just couldn't find the positive driving force to hang onto. The only joy I had at this point was the actual martial arts sessions themselves. There was a sense of release while I was learning how to block, and strike during sparring sessions. This was the same relief I experienced back when I was still on basketball or softball teams. For me, the challenge of being a part of a team was a very rewarding experience. It was one of the few times that I felt like I really belonged to something and mattered.

As the struggle intensified; I crossed another lost soul who was probably just as lost as myself, and one night we decided to break in to the back of a local business. Upon our youthful ignorance, we found ourselves trapped for about an hour until finally wedging the door back open and escaping without being caught.

From there, I ran home and tried to explain to my mother what I had done, and for days building up to that point, I was in and out of trouble. I was just about to turn 16, and here I landed myself on a very strict set of circumstances doled out from my mother. I wasn't allowed to leave the house, and I wasn't given any privileges. My thoughts then ran amok; I spent periods of inner agony rocking in place and bawling uncontrollably. My mind raced and struggled to alleviate the obvious suffering for which I had to face alone. I hid the pain from my mother, I didn't want her to know how deeply I hurt moreover that she didn't blame herself. In truth; I had some deep sorrow from witnessing my parents fighting and watching our family fall apart in the way that it had. this was a pattern I began to sense as *normal* though I often questioned this method of thinking. I would notice other kids happily existing with their parents who seemed to really have love for another.

Love ... An emotion that I never used to know firsthand nor experienced.

There was no doubt that my family loved me. My extended family also loved me; aunts, uncles, grandparents, great-grandparents. Both of my parents had better moments of loving me enough to a point that I kind of understood it, but, it was something that I felt like I lost sight of about the time my parents divorced. I could see love between my mother and her new partner, and my father with his, but I wasn't feeling it myself. Perhaps I was too lost to the depression, or moreover, the recognition that I was being bullied and ridiculed on a regular basis. This began to build as the obsessive belief that perhaps I just wasn't capable of being loved. This was obviously a foolish mistake.

Due to my mother's restrictions; I jumped out of a second story window one night and ran away from home which began my downward spiral into the cruelty of reality. Fueled with alcohol and cigarettes, I bounce around from house to house a while before crossing some kids from school who were renting an apartment together. I show up with the money my father had given me for child support and took on residence in an apartment filled with other troubled teenagers.

There was no control to be had in this new existence. If ever I was grossly misguided; that was indeed the moment of my adolescent life where I had made the worst judgments and biggest mistakes. That was the period at the young age of 16 where I assumed I was now an adult - what a *destructive* mode of thinking.

With no rules nor adult supervision; this apartment turned into a partying mayhem with all of the weed and alcohol included. It astounds me looking back at how many older men were so readily willing to buy the alcohol for young teenage girls. There wasn't a care or concern in the world from these men, but rather, they viewed it as a collection of easy targets they could manipulate for their sexual desires.

14

As I think back today; I'd give anything I could to go back and change a lot of my own mistakes and otherwise bad judgments. If ever that became an option, I would talk more openly to my mother and stay at home with her to work on the situations that I was struggling with.

If I could tell any teenager anything about that period in my life, it would be to look at my struggles and realize where my destructive choices had led me astray. I spent most of my life trapped and in a lot of pain and wasn't able to fully succeed whereas if I had stayed with my mother, I would have been a hell of a lot more successful and productive. I went many years trapped in something that I couldn't escape and most of my bad choices paved that road. Am I partly guilty? Yes I am. I had the power to stop this destructive behavior at any time but I continued down this road of self destruction and chaos blind to what I was really doing to myself. I essentially set myself up to fail. Something that I highly regret.

It is important to remember that you do have the power to change your life at any time. Recognize the problem and identify with it. Chances are, you can receive help and find more productive ways of coping with anything you might be going through. All of us were angry teenagers at some point ... All of us have made those bad choices that led us down the wrong path. I have yet to meet somebody who can honestly say they haven't screwed up at some point or another while growing up - part of growing up into adulthood does consist of falling sometimes but then learning how to stand up all over again and knowing that you can if you just try.

Strangers would continue to show up and bring beer and weed and among that crowd was a more persistent one who failed to acknowledge I was still only 16 years old. He was smart enough to gain my attention with promises of never running out of cigarettes or beer. To my polluted existence; this was an ideally perfect promise that would ensure that I could continue on the downward spiral without worrying of denying myself of those useless needs.

One important thing any teenage girl should remember is that some men will say or do anything to gain your affection. They will use any lies or means available to them to win you over and the ones who prey on underage girls know how easy it is to fool one. They are usually well versed in flattery and even the current music; they will know what to say, how to say it, and use empty promises and even money. It is especially important for young girls to be aware and educated on the dangers that lurk behind those lies and promises. I understand how it feels to be a lost and lonely teen trying to find out who you are. You're insecure, nobody takes you serious, you're depressed, you're lost, confused, you think you know it all, the kids at school are cruel and petty, you feel like nobody listens to you, you think you have to have name brand anything to fit in, your parents are annoying to you, you aren't allowed to go to parties every time you ask, all you really want is attention and love ... *I get it*. But know there are other ways to handle this than alcohol, drugs or seeking it from potential predators. Be inspiring. Pick up art, a hobby perhaps, ignore the haters, avoid social media if that becomes painful for you, talk to trusted people, they're out there! Whatever you do, do not act out on revenge against your parents or pure impulse.

Life is hard, and I know it firsthand and lived it. What all of us really want the most is to be loved and understood and free to be who we are without criticism or judgment. Always remember this: There will always be people who will judge you or criticize you whoever you are and whatever you do. If you want to surpass that, show the haters and common naysayer that you're unaffected and in time they will see how strong and beautiful you really are. There is nothing more attractive than someone who is comfortable in their own skin loaded with positive confidence. They will drown in envy and even be afraid of you because they don't know how to be comfortable with themselves.

What should have been a red flag had come up next when I agreed to go with him to his place to party. There was a houseful of others who were also drinking as well as a familiar face; a girl I had gone to school with but didn't know so well. Because I recognized her, I kind of felt a degree of comfort but that would soon diminish when I made it known that I wanted to return home. Later that next day I had plans on attending a friend's bridal shower with my mother, something I had been looking forward to for weeks.

As I left on foot, this seemed to really anger him and he took it upon himself to follow me down the road. This really began to concern me as I had no other intention than to go sober up and attend the bridal shower in friendly company.

His anger began to flow out as he began swatting at me and hitting me. At the time, I was overcoming a walking pneumonia and on my person I carried the antibiotics. In an attempt to defend myself, I threw the bottle at him and the pills scattered across the road. This actually caused him to step back and pick them up and as he had, I changed direction. My original plan was to make it to my father's house which was a few minutes down the road. It would have been quicker and more efficient for me to reach his house as opposed to walking all the way from that location to the village of Chittenango. He however struggled to prevent me at all costs. Here I was just 16 years old with this angry 24 year old man bruising me and hitting me. It was a real scary and troublesome moment that should of said "run as fast as you can!" and I had an actual fear for my life assuming he would be just crazy enough to throw me in front of a passing car. I wasn't sure that I would make it, but luckily a friend of his surfaced and continued the walk with me to the village.

This is a very important part of my own story where I have to make you, the reader see my personal mistake. At that time, I stupidly believed I really liked him and I wanted him to feel the same in return. I believed that I *needed* the feelings returned that I possessed for him. Though I knew his actions were very out of hand, I chose to ignore the warning. I convinced myself that perhaps the next day, he wouldn't be that abusive and maybe I had made the mistake of leaving and I had at that moment set myself up for what would continue through the entire relationship - blaming myself for something that wasn't my fault at all.

If you are someplace with others, you should be able to own the choice for yourself to leave if you wanted to. In no way should you ever sacrifice what *you* ultimately want. Another problem was that the use of violence was his means of trying to control me into staying. You are not someone's property and nobody owns any right to tell you what you can or cannot do. Also, do not ever let someone make you feel like you did something wrong by simply desiring to leave. Making personal choices such as the decision to leave a party doesn't mean you are hurting anyone. It simply means you had enough and you want to go home.

Eventually, I finally settle back the apartment after the long walk from North Chittenango and my mother shows up and notices the numerous marks and bruises on me. At this point, I was in too much pain and had an immeasurable amount of exhaustion from the abuse and extended walk and wanted to fall asleep. However, my mother was persistent and had me report the situation to the Chittenango police.

During that moment I decidedly listened to her, and I sat down with an officer explaining what had happened and also showed him the marks and from there they had gone out to make the arrest.

My biggest mistake in this situation is that these troubling events should have been a big booming voice screaming to stay well away from him, but because of my addictions and other misguiding thoughts, I went back into court later and perjured myself by claiming to have made a false statement. My mother knew better. His friend knew better ... The kids I was staying with definitely knew better and they even told me I was making a mistake. In the negative pattern of thinking in which I was lost into, I went against my better judgment and set myself up for more pain and depression. In hindsight, I can tell you that I didn't know any better. I believed this is how you loved and this is how love feels; a series of tears, fists and name-calling while feeling like a meaningless shell of existence who was better off dead.

With the 8 year age difference, and the recognition of what he was actually capable of; neither of my parents were pleased when I eventually moved from the house-to-house bouncing to his home in North Chittenango.

Just weeks before moving in with him; other so-called friends dragged me along to a party out in North Syracuse. This specific party was loaded with men of many ages equipped with liquor and weed. All of the typical things I had come to be surrounded by during my very young existence.

The friend who asked me to follow her ultimately abandoned me in this house with people I didn't know and the outcome is something I have never talked about to anyone before sitting down to write this book. As I said, the party had a lot of guys at various ages and after the other women left, they brought me down to the basement and took advantage of my inability to defend myself. Each of them took a turn at raping me to the point I had passed out unconscious. I remember feeling terrified and unable to break free as they took turns. During some of it, I would pass out while I struggled and I cried out for them to stop, but it continued nevertheless to the point that the aftermath threw me into the belief that I was completely emotionally dead. Now I was completely conditioned into a thought pattern that convinced me that I was born to be hurt, raped, hit and thrown away. How could I have believed anything else? That was all I knew.

When I later confronted the person who abandoned me, she fully denied doing so and tried to place all of the blame on me. If you've ever been in a position similar to mine, I hope you know that in no way is it your fault. At no point is a beautiful girl or woman asking for this sort of treatment and at no point should anyone ever take advantage of you as it is the most disgusting and cruel act anyone could ever do to another. I want you to also remember that if your friend abandons you when it was promised they wouldn't, that is not a friend at all, but rather somebody you don't need in your life. A real friend would never leave you behind; they would do anything to honor their promise.

That rape took away my sense of self, of who I am, my dreams, my security. The situations leading to that point weren't much better and they also played a huge role in my mental decline but it was that aftermath of rape that truly destroyed me. I was being blamed, I was being ridiculed and I was told I was worthless. The shame that I felt thereafter was so profound that it permeated my every thought in which I turned to music as a way to alleviate the pain. Music, alcohol, and weed; the building blocks of destructive thinking and behavior.

After moving in with the 24 year old; it wasn't long before I was pregnant. My father took the news harshly as any father would. He refused to speak with me and this killed me. I needed both of my parents now more than ever. I had just went through this series of abusive situations and now I began to feel really stuck with this older guy who has a 'fly on the handle' bad temper.

Between his noticeable outbursts, things were okay. Just, okay. I wasn't actually happy nor did I feel love from him but at this point, I figured now I have his child and so I have to make the best of this very bad situation.

His family is pretty large as he had numerous brothers and sisters. Like my school days, I really sorely wanted to belong. It was a need that kind of overcame my ability to realize I was really just stuck in a real bad situation that I could of easily left at any time. By appearance, the siblings seemed to get along with another and I have to be honest in stating that family values did exist. The one brother already had kids and it was a joy to sometimes watch them interact. I saw in the brother's family a reminder of the comfort of my childhood when my parents got along. It was a minor, but acceptable form of normalcy that I clung onto with all I was worth. A big part of me wanted to be around them more than anything and at every chance made possible.

As before, it wasn't long before that brother would secretly make sexual advances towards me. What this began to identify to me was that apparently all I am good for is sex and that is all anyone seems to want from me, sex. He had this beautiful woman at his side; someone whom I actually looked up to and gravitated towards because she seemed to have a very stable and motherly personality. It deeply disgusted me that the brother would try to pursue me, I actually loathed him for it and felt truly sorry for her. In no way did I want further blame for something that wouldn't be my fault at all; much less did I want her to dislike me for something that I wasn't even doing so I remained at a safe enough distance to avoid any sort of misunderstanding.

At gatherings; these brothers and friends would brag about group sex and other illicit activities that really deeply disgusted me. Though I knew nothing but abuse and pain, there was still the rational and practical side of me who knew there was something very wrong here. I'd listen to their foolish babble while sat in a corner quietly - I feared that one of them would turn at any moment, and I wasn't about to risk that. My goal was to simply fit in, and what a battle that had become.

If you have ever heard the term 'wolf-packing' and didn't quite understand what that meant, you're not alone. I too never heard of the term, much less understood it until coming into this group of people. Wolf-packing is an event where three or more people gang up on one person. In this circle; if you disagreed with anything or did something that triggered one of them, you got pounced by the entire group. A certain method that would scare anyone into a dark corner to hide. Something else I considered when I first sat down to tell my story - I understood that by telling *my* story, someone in the crowd would assume the right to try and bully me out of it. They would do or say anything to scare me away from talking about the situations and circumstances in which I lived through before finally breaking free. I want you to know that at no moment as of so far have I let any such thing deter me from what I am doing, which is telling my story in a way to help others.

By telling such a complex story; I knew that it would take uncovering some of my own faults, mistakes and downfalls because in truth ... not one of us are ever perfect or perfectly innocent. In the mindset that I was trapped in, it would be indeed inhuman not to have made some incredible mistakes along the way. I know by releasing this novel that people will learn some things about me that they may not have known before but it ought to be acknowledged that I am brave enough, strong enough, and proud enough to be honest and admit to my own faults. That is something that a lot of people could not, nor would not ever do.

As I began to learn the inner workings of this family, I began to accept its unusual behaviors and activities. It was quite a feat at that period of time to persuade my own mind into assuming that this has got to be normal. Funny that despite all of the depression and bullying; I was incredibly brainwashed and yet I somehow subconsciously understood that none of this was at all normal.

If ever there is something within you that is telling you that something is wrong, chances are that it is wrong and you should maybe listen. But, how many of us actually ignore our intuition and gut instinct? Especially at the very impressionable age of just 16 years old, you're not truly exposed to the world fully and there is a lot going on within you. Personally speaking; by 16 I was confused, depressed, obsessed, and even troubled and in no way should I have ever sought out comfort in the ways that I had. Anyone reading this however knows that when you are a troubled teen, nothing much is really getting through to you and you are really quite blind. I know I certainly was. Not only was I extremely intelligent, but I was driven solely by a deep desire to just belong. A terrible and frightening place for a teen to be.

There were people who really did try to direct me to the right path. People from my martial arts courses, aunts, friends of the family, uncles, grandparents. Their words (although true) would go in one ear and right out of the other. I was certain that I had life figured out and nobody was going to tell me different, not even my own inner voices.

As the baby grew inside of me, I was conscious enough of the new life although a kid myself, and decidedly stopped drinking altogether. I recall periods of withdrawal from the use of alcohol but also consciously prioritized the helpless life growing inside of me. As concerning the 24 year old father (whom I will refer to in this story as the 'abuser'), I knew I had no real feelings for him whatsoever - I began trying to force myself to at least feel a hint of love as an attempt to accept that he is fathering my unborn child. It was something I worked through and failed at during the two decades I spent trapped with him. The love I was trying to force myself to feel was a sacrifice of my true feelings for the sake of our child. I knew how I felt when my parents divorced and separated, and how that made me feel deep down. In no way was I even considering putting my own baby through that.

Despite my renewed sense of life and considerations for a baby not yet here, his excitement was rather minimal. Most expectant fathers (or so I believed) would be glowing in excitement much like I noticed recently in my own brother when he and his lovely wife had their first child.

The abuser seemed burdened and troubled by the pregnancy and often argued with me and left the home.

One fight I recall, it had escalated to the point of where he had shoved me back and swung at me, and in return I actually stuck a lit cigarette on his face near his left eye. My retaliation was that of fear and memory of the earlier attacks - I had this new life growing in me, and I wanted to defend it at all costs. Do I now regret that situation? I am not pleased with myself for some of my reactions to the abuse, but

I knew I had to defend myself somehow. By using a cigarette in defense, I knew the heat of the lit end would be enough to prevent him from escalating more violently. In my mind, I assumed it would slow him down to see what he was doing. Will I tell you that I was in the right for doing such a thing? No. Nobody in any sort of relationship should ever have to resort to such extreme measures whatsoever. This took me a long time to come to terms with, but, there is no existence of actual love when so much hurt and pain is involved. Again, another red flag that I turned a blind eye to.

The arguments and altercations verbal and otherwise escalated throughout the pregnancy. I came to believe that in no way did he really want this child and I came to expect more and more jabs and blows. Something that I am still convinced today is an accurate view of the situation.

By my 6th month in, I noticed some pain and discomfort that went beyond just normal cramping or growing pains. I found it hard to walk, much less get out of bed. My energetic youthfulness however prevented me from understanding what might had been going on. During several doctor exams, I was assured that things were okay and that the pregnancy is going along as it should. I was never given instructions to rest or take it easy, and therefore went on doing normal activities such as walking around town.

Just into my 7th month; we were driving an old Bonneville over to a store in the middle of Chittenango village. I can't remember exactly why he was upset, but he began smashing me into the dash of the car and spitting anger at me. I tried to prevent him from repeatedly smashing me into that dash but he wouldn't stop. I was eventually pinned and I could feel this extremely painful tearing sensation go up through the left side of my stomach. I flailed myself around in an attempt to struggle free but the pain was so severe that I nearly passed out. A moment later, a Chittenango cop had opened the door and pulled him out of the driver's side of the car preventing him from harming me further. Without hesitation, the cop brought him to the police car and instructed me to go home. As instructed, I drove myself home in fear of the pain and discomfort I was experiencing.

Some time later he returned and of course tried to convince me that somehow that altercation was my fault and that I deserved it. I couldn't figure out what the hell I did to deserve that sort of treatment, but he persistently told me that it was all my fault then later apologized and promised it would never happen again.

In the weeks that followed, he used what was called party lines to meet other people. In the mid-1990's, there was a call center that was similar to an internet chat room where you called a phone number, and got connected to other people in your area and had conversations with them much like you would see in an internet chat room. He used this system while I would be asleep to talk with other women whom he intended to meet. What he didn't know what that I was well aware of what he was doing but pretended to be naive enough to not realize he was looking for gullible women to sleep with. At this stage of the relationship, the fact that he was actively often trying to sleep with other women really bothered me and took a serious toll on my self-esteem. Here I was pregnant at 16 with his child, and going through a series of abusive situations while he was praising these strange women for anything possible to get in their good graces. In one such situation, the girl he was trying to bed had actually approached me and told me exactly what he said and how he claimed to be single and available. She explained that once she realized who he was and that I was carrying his child, she removed herself from any further contact and would have nothing more to do with him. This truth coming to light was but another red flag I was blind to.

I turn 17 and the baby is due soon. The partying around me continued non-stop. His family members and friends in and out of the new apartment without a care in the world or concern for me or my pregnancy.

Though some painful blows occurred in-between; the event during that first pregnancy that I remember the most was the late-afternoon in the beginning of August. Again, I can't honestly tell you how that argument began, but what I can tell you is that it escalated rather quickly. I remember trying to defend myself and my unborn child, but as he progressed rapidly in anger, he finally snapped and slammed me through a kitchen chair and down onto an industrial tile floor that met me with a striking blow.

In a matter of days, the pain in my stomach was so severe that I could barely stand it. With no understanding of what to expect during pregnancy, I called a nurse from my gynecologist's office. Through a thick of tears, I explained that I had ran a bath and it was filling with blood. The nurse on the other end of the phone had just assumed I was naive. She insisted that I was having Braxton-hicks contractions and shouldn't be alarmed nor worried. Her suggestion because of her lack of understanding just how much blood I was losing was simply: "Until you are covered from head to toe in blood, you do not need to come in here."

The pain and the flow of blood was just unbearable so by ignoring the nurse's crass instruction, I asked a friend to drive me to the hospital.

Upon initial examination, the hospital nurse was beside herself. I was asked to change out of my underwear for an exam and a plethora of blood fell out of me. From there, I was immediately admitted and set up for examination. As the friend who had given me a ride waited patiently downstairs in the lobby, the doctor had ordered for an ultrasound to be given. Unaware of what I was due to hear next, I lie in this bed in a pool of tears and pain realizing that I hadn't felt the baby move in days - not since the night I was slammed down to the floor through a kitchen chair that folded beneath me as my body was thrown into it.

The ultrasound technicians spend about 5 minutes or so with me before leaving the examination room. 10 minutes later ... The doctor comes in and looks at me with a straight, unemotional face and calmly recited the words that forever haunted me "your baby has no heartbeat."

...

My mind took at least a minute to register those five words as I had now realized that my unborn child had died inside of my body in the womb - possibly a direct result from the violent altercation that occurred just days prior. Was this a red flag? Yes. Was I blind? Very. That day was the first day of my struggle with Post Traumatic Stress Disorder; a day that has haunted me then and even today as I sit here and write. If I thought I had depression before, that was indeed the moment where it was introduced to me in buckets full of darkness that poured over and submerged me into a flowing river of desolation. That day, a large part of me died, and along with it, my sense of being. There was so much of my life up to that point which had went wrong, and losing that first child was the force that shoved me far off the edge and left me to drown. The days to follow; I had very serious thoughts of dying in my sleep. I'd pray through the night begging God to take me away from what I believed I was really caught in. A forever stretch of hopeless night ...

Chapter 2

"Grief can't be shared. Everyone carries it alone.
His own burden in his own way."

~ Anne Morrow Lindbergh

The loss of a child is probably one of the most painful and traumatic situations any parent should never have to experience nor understand. Doing it alone however is exceedingly worse. I was left to the dark thoughts of my mind and absolutely nobody to talk them out to. I went through the motions of wondering what I could have done different to blaming myself because I *knew* he was violent and that wasn't changing. I wanted to run away but didn't know where to run. I wanted to die but I didn't even have the courage. All I had left of my baby was a cedar box adorned with a crucifix filled with the ashes of a child I'll never get to see grow up. It was an extreme low-point of my young life that set me up for the long-term entrapment.

My grief was so severe that I constantly cried and stayed in bed day and night. In his lack of empathy; he'd ridicule and laugh at me while I was made to witness his affections for other women. It was like he didn't care that his own child would never grow up or be a person. He didn't really show grief after the funeral and sometimes now I question what little grief he did exhibit. In truth, I do believe that he played the part of a grieving father for his family and whoever else would be in attendance during the calling hours. In fact, emotions were something he could call upon when he needed any sort of attention. Nothing rakes in more attention from other women than a man who is crying and appears to need help with his mourning process. Undoubtedly, a pathetic stunt performed by a very shallow and heartless individual. The only people I can think of who would even consider doing something that shallow are narcissists and what better way to feed themselves than with an excuse such as a loss to fill those selfish needs.

In time, my grief lessoned and I was able to function well enough to at least get out of bed and attempt to move on. My struggle however continued as I would sometimes faintly hear a baby crying late into the night. The presence of this audible experience made me feel like I was close to madness while I'd wonder if perhaps I really was losing my mind. When I had mentioned to him that I could hear the cries of an infant, he not only had a lack of concern, but he went out of his way to cut me down and ridicule me by stating I was a 'hysterical bitch' and 'insane'.

Certainly, I had spent an immeasurable amount of time with guilt and while I now recollect, it's easy to see why my mind could have conjured those audible hallucinations.

The traumatic grief was served to me in handfuls as I was barely able to make any real progress. When I was lucky enough to fall asleep, I would relive the afternoon that he smashed me through the chair and onto the floor. The emotional detachment from everyone including my own mother soon followed. Any optimism that I once had was completely awash as now; a bitter sense of utter hopelessness dangled before me and cloaked that scintilla of hope with absolute darkness. I was now numb.

I kept reliving the first hours after giving birth to my dead child, even while trying to watch television or trying to focus on something else. From puzzles to word-searches; those hours lingered in my mind.

Post-birth; they removed the baby from the hospital room, and brought her back to me shortly after. The nurse responsible for cleaning her up didn't do the best job and so the abuser demanded that they cleaned her a little better before handing her to me. The nurse complied, and then brought me a dead baby; my baby, whom I had named Amanda. A child that I had excitedly anticipated raising. They had her dressed and wrapped in a receiving blanket much like they would a living newborn. When they handed the baby to me, I was so dead on the inside that I sat there emotionless while I held her. He rambled on about how the nurse hadn't done such a great job cleaning her the first time but all I could think about was how he was the one responsible for this child who will never get to experience life. He was the sole reason why I had to give birth to a stillborn baby and he failed to acknowledge that. While I may had seemed emotionless on the outside, I was in a fiery rage within. I could have told one of them, or even my mother but he'd never admit to it and I knew that. Quietly I sat nearly catatonic holding the results of what had come from staying in an abusive relationship.

What I want to talk about now are some key points that you should consider and I will first start with the grief and ridicule.

If you are reading this, perhaps you have one time been in my position or are currently there and you want to understand what to do. While conceiving how to approach writing this book, I spent a great amount of time thinking about what I really wanted to get across as a way to help others who may feel trapped in a bad situation. I have survived a lot over the two decades (I will point out key parts) and I will discuss not just the situations, but also my thoughts and how I had come to realize that I did not deserve what he was doing to me and that I could and eventually would get out.

His inability to share compassion and understanding should have been the sole driving force for my leaving the relationship. When I left that hospital, I should have left with my mother and I should have told her what had happened that day he had slammed me through the chair.

Certainly there are a lot of people who will not understand why I hadn't run fast and far - any woman living in such duress isn't ever understood by a lot of people and that is because they haven't lived in the same situation and therefore they cannot truly understand it. Up to the point where I had lost my child, he was steadily conditioning me and reprogramming me by way of continued insults and use of violent force. I understood that what he was doing to me was wrong, but I was also a very depressed teen by the time I had crossed him so what he really did was take full advantage of me at a time in my life where I wasn't really sure what love was or how personal relationships were meant to be.

No teenager can really fully understand as they have not yet had a chance to really live life. They're just out of the role of playful child and growing into the stages of a young adult. Take a teenager without guidance and you have a recipe for many mistakes to occur. I had no idea what to really expect out of life and what I should do outside of attending high school and graduating. Take the absence of help from the school out of the equation and now you can sort of get an idea of how I believed that I was left alone to face this storm.

I couldn't truly see the beast for what it was, so I resorted to the assumption that this was as good as it gets. One of the biggest mistakes that anyone in an abusive relationship will make is to settle for what they have while trying to avoid any type of conflict. As I mentioned above; I cannot to this day remember what it was that triggered him into slamming me through that kitchen chair. For all I know, it may had been as simple as arguing over affording a pack of cigarettes or perhaps even food. Sometimes that is all it takes to trigger these enormous bursts of anger; a simple and small situation that you couldn't possibly be at fault for.

If you are with a partner, and you both have lost a child; he as the expectant father should be right at your side grieving with you. In no way should you ever be made to feel inadequate or crazy while you go through the motions - certainly we all grieve differently and we may sometimes desire to be alone but we also need a healthy support group to work through the trauma from the sudden and unexpected loss. In his case, he was too busy seeking out other women and drinking and was absent for much of the time. He made no effort to exhibit an ounce of compassion for me, but would only appear to if and when another man was around.

The isolation was alarming; any attempt I made to speak with anyone also triggered him so he would use the method of accusing me or suggesting that the friend was up to no good and only trying to cause trouble.

The last thing on my mind was other men or the like. You don't go from losing your child to the desire of sex with other men, it's illogical and telling on his part. Not only did he lack the support for my grief but he went out of his way to isolate me from any sort of real support.

I began to see my 5 year old self out there in the field at the tree with the rabbit, butterflies and dragonflies. They're looking back at me with sad eyes while behind me approaches this tempestuous storm that cannot be slowed or redirected. The butterflies quickly disappear and the dragonflies follow just behind them while the rabbit takes one last look at me before proceeding towards the clearing where there's sun and tranquil peace - this is my mind telling me that if I walk back into the storm, I will remain isolated. If however I had followed the rabbit, I would have been free from the isolation and continued turmoil. I wanted to follow the rabbit but I felt like I had chains wrapped around me and they began yanking me back into the darkness. I struggled and tried to get loose but the hold was too tight to break free from. All of the color was washed away from my vision and now I was adrift in a pool of utter darkness. There was one very small glimmer of light in the distance and a singular monarch just above my head as I was quickly sinking - that significance of hope was just enough to convince me to keep my head above water before becoming completely submerged.

It was eventual with his apparent sexual desires that I was once again pregnant. Barely three months had passed between the loss and moment of conception. The shock of the traumatic loss was still evident and I was barely given a real chance to grieve or surpass the bereavement process. This second conception wasn't received in happiness, but rather torment. It became a very real fear to once again endure 9 months with the thought that perhaps I would lose another baby in the same way that I had lost the first.

As a result of his continued inability to recognize his part in the loss; he deemed it necessary to direct me to a new doctor and hospital and began placing blame where it wasn't deserved. My focus was neither on the doctor nor the hospital, but rather if he will get angry enough to once again lash out at me while carrying this new baby. I had lost all sense of trust with anyone and began to close in while keeping to myself. Out of all of the things I have survived in my lifetime, I can honestly say to you that there is nothing more terrifying than to wonder if you'll get hit hard enough to lose your baby. My oldest son will never truly know the struggle I went through mentally while carrying him those long and seemingly endless 40 weeks. The fear was intoxicating, crippling, and even numbing. The continued nightmares of the day my doctor told me that my baby had no heartbeat haunted me - while going for sonograms, I cringed at the thought that those very words would be repeated. The other and more prominent fear was that at any moment, he may snap and bludgeon me or kick me or maybe even slam me through something else. This was the sort of nightmare that set me up into total confinement within myself. Without the ability to trust anyone, I was left completely unable to relay these types of thoughts and so I was lost to a fear that overtook my mind.

In the OBGYN waiting room with other expectant mothers, I watched at a quiet distance while the expectant fathers would lovingly embrace them and talk with them with so much light in their eyes. Their joy as I saw it was profoundly overwhelming and beautiful. Inside I was crying as I observed what I could have had if I wasn't so caught up in the abusive relationship with a man who cared only about himself. The love that I observed was nothing like anything I had ever known and in a way it inspired me. I wanted that excitement with a partner, and I wanted to know what it felt like to be appreciated and cared for. My thoughts began to manifest a fictitious partner; one I would often visit in my dreams as a way to cope with my lack thereof. This was no substitute for what I longed for, but it was enough to wade the storm with my head just above the water.

So, what is real love compared to the illusion of love? It has taken me a very long time to differentiate between the two, but as of so far, this is what I have come to learn: Currently, I am in a relationship with a man who puts my needs before his own. There is a mutual understanding between us as well as a bond derived from surviving very abusive relationships. He is neither selfish nor angry; but rather patient, understanding and compassionate. Instead of screaming and blame-games, there is a compromise met with a mutual agreement in which maintains peace within the household. The time we spend together is cherished and looked forward to without fear or wondering what will trigger an outburst or rage. There exists no insults nor put-downs and there is total and complete trust that is never lost to either of us. Making love is not a chore nor forced, it is a natural occurrence that becomes a magical moment which is mutually shared. When something doesn't work as it should or it breaks down, I am not blamed for the faulty mechanics, but rather assisted in a combined effort to alleviate the problem. When I cry, he wipes away my tears and often feels the pain I am experiencing and cries with me. We embrace another and lovingly erase the woes together.

Real love is neither forced nor meant to be painful. By definition; real love varies between us but what most people can tell you is that it would never harm you and it never makes you feel like you can't do anything right. With my current relationship; the love came naturally as it should. He didn't just show up and take advantage of me in my weakened state. There wasn't a point where I felt like I had to force him to care for me, it just naturally occurred. For those of us who have felt like we had to find a way to make our partner love us, to have it happen natural is very foreign territory but I assure you that not only can it happen, but it is equal to discovering heaven on earth (at least in my opinion.)

In the illusion of love, you are constantly trying to be good enough and are cautious not to make any mistakes. You worry about others being your competition and wonder what you can do to be worthy enough to win his affections. Honestly, it is like living a lie; there is no possibility to actually make anyone love you. You may want to believe that if you make a serious effort that perhaps he would see how hard you are trying and somehow love you enough to treat you as an equal instead of a lesser. With any abuse present in the relationship; it is hard to understand why it is happening to you and you will want to blame yourself. He may be saying he is sorry after each fight and claiming to love you but the sobering truth is that it's a ploy on his behalf to simply manipulate and control you. When I first lost the baby, he said he was sorry though I was spared from hearing "it will never happen again" because he didn't have the guts to own up to what he had done. I heard him say "I love you" but in no way could that bring my baby daughter back. I wanted to believe that maybe he would change when I conceived my oldest son, I wanted it more then than ever but deep down I actually knew that there was no way I was going to see any change. His days of lying about that much were indeed over but because I was afraid of what he was capable of, I kept that to myself and began to go through the motions like a programmed drone doing as I was told.

When I finally gave birth to my oldest son; the relief of his being born healthy took a little bit of the weight off of my constant worry over losing another child the way I had the first one. As I held him for the first time, I was awash with overwhelming emotion. Here was this little helpless life given to me from God who would depend on me and love me unconditionally without viewing me as the mistake or failure. This also bestowed a surreal sense of new panic and anxiety as I also knew that I would be singularly the sole entity to give care and love to this new helpless life. My fear of not being enough once again heightened though I pressed forward with just enough self confidence to provide whatever I could for my newborn child.

The other factor that weighed in was also that I felt completely stuck with the abuser as now we have a child in common. Being the legal father, he would have rights to the baby so that realization crippled me from even considering looking into ways of escaping the relationship. I was still very much a child myself; I was barely 18 and hardly able to take the best care of myself or even know how to survive in society without someone there to guide me. What I did understand was that it would take money which meant a job, and it would take locking down a trusted babysitter and that was where I failed to conceive a plan. I was already stuck in the mindset of assuming that I could never trust anyone so why would I risk placing my newborn child with anyone other than myself if I wasn't able to trust.

Here's the truth about controlling and manipulative abusers. They are consistent with keeping you away from people you may have once trusted as a way to keep a good hold on you. They know that not everyone will buy their facade and realize that a family member or a good friend will try to help you out of the situation. What they may not understand is that by isolating you from people who used to be constant in your life, those people will begin to realize that there is something not quite right and will not give up trying to figure out what that might be. The one person in my life who knew better was my mother. She had experienced similar circumstances herself and therefore she knew that despite even what I was saying, there was something very wrong.

The grief was taking a toll on me still after the birth of my son. I tried to focus on his needs and maintain the juggling emotions that entwined themselves around the worsening depression. Without the proper time to grieve and without any support, my inside battles went from bad to worse. This began to develop into a familiar theme of my life.

With a constant flow of troubling situations varying from gang rape, bullying, facing loneliness to having my baby beaten out of me; this greatly diminished any sense of hope or even the desire to be happy. With this type of conditioning, I unfortunately settled and learned how to lie to my questioning mother to spare myself any further trauma. I had indeed become careless for myself but the last thing I wanted was for my son to know pain in the way that I had come to know it.

My mother still questioned him despite and because she was persistent, I received the brunt of her inquisitions. He would try to dissuade me from her by suggesting that all that she wanted was our baby. He wanted me to turn against her because he knew that she was not falling for any of his lies or tall stories he'd produce. She was undoubtedly a threat for him - someone who wasn't buying into his web of fabrication. To spare myself from him, I called her and visited as little as possible. The resentment I had within for him was profound. Not only has he taken my baby but he was as well taking everyone in my life away from me. He was stranding me in a position where the only person I was allowed to interact with was only him and my newborn son.

I needed my family, and I missed them but as the time slowly passed, I began to believe that I was the unwanted family member. They were no longer in my life and now I was becoming surrounded by only his family. There existed nothing but continued negativity, drug use, partying, conflict, aggravation and them constantly ganging up on me. If it wasn't him going at me, then it was one of them and they were fond of the constant turmoil.

My thoughts at the time of the prolonged grief had a lot to do with blaming myself. I knew I should of had him banned from the hospital because I knew deep down he was the cause but I was scared that nobody would listen to me. After all, I was still a teenager and who would take a troubled teen serious right?
Wrong.

It doesn't matter how old you are or what you're going through, do not let those thoughts derived from fear stop you from speaking up. I can tell you from experience that people do know and they will listen to you. I don't care how hard he tries to convince you that nobody will believe you, people know a hell of a lot more than you give them credit for. What I have learned from my situation is that people who abuse others will try awful hard to look good and will always be flawed in doing so. They may fool a handful, but not everyone. If you've ever heard the saying "the truth always comes out" take it serious. A person abusing you or controlling you will try to dupe you into thinking that nobody will believe you. They do so by belittling you and making you feel inferior and worthless but I want you to remember something; you matter. You are worthy. You are not the problem and you do not deserve to get hurt no matter what he says you've done wrong. When you are in a relationship with somebody, you deserve to be loved and treated with respect. Sometimes couples argue over money, and there may even be a hint of jealousy here or there, let's face it, life happens! Sometimes you may disagree with your partner and that is okay. But if the disagreement is always pinned on you and you are made to feel like a mistake, don't allow yourself to believe it. That's what these men want you to do, believe that it is you and not them.

My biggest mistake *was* my silence - in a way that also puts me at fault and I am unafraid to admit that to anyone. Looking back at the loss of my baby; my thoughts were all over the place. The depth of personal guilt was so intoxicating that I was literally drowning in it. When I first discovered I was pregnant, I briefly considered an abortion because I knew that he was abusive. I also had aspirations of going back to school and moving on to higher education. In the back of my mind, I knew that if I kept the baby, it would tie me to him and there was a part of me who wanted to pursue a career and return back to school. Through the entire pregnancy I had endured the violence and mental abuse and that should have been my wake up call. One of the biggest problems I recognized in my own situation was that I even began to lie for him. For example; my mother would ask me what was really going on and I would cover up the truth as much as I could even though she knew better. By doing this, I was literally enabling him to continue this behavior and that is a mistake I feel that a lot of people in this situation will make. Do not think that people aren't able to see through the facade. You may want them to believe that everything is okay but despite your efforts, they are going to see the truth.

This abusive illusion of love is an instance where you may want to believe that you have it. As I mentioned in the first chapter, I was a lonely and depressed individual and one of the things I wanted the most was acceptance. That desire to have just that helped my mind build up the illusion which is one of the most destructive I could have ever done to myself. By building this illusion, I disabled my own ability to see something for what it really is. I wanted to believe and I wanted to convince myself that things were okay when they really weren't. At that point of my young life, the only thing I thought I had known about love was that abuse came with it. What I saw with my parents should have been moreover a lesson as to what not to get trapped into.

We have all met those people who blame their every mistake on their childhood, those people who sit and say that because they had it so bad, that is why they are in and out of jail or whatever it is they're going through. I'm not one of those people. As we grow up, the first people in our lives during our most impressionable years are our families to include parents, brothers, sisters, aunts, uncles, ect. I do agree that our personalities are shaped around what we are surrounded by; however, as we grow into young adults, we do have a mind of our own and we do know right from wrong.

My mother recently had a conversation with me in which she reminded me of when I said to her that I would never let myself live through what she had. In no way was my father a monster, but he had his share of issues. I watched her go through years of trying to get free from the marriage and ultimately succeeding. If anything, that should have been the one thing that prevented me from making the same mistakes and yet it didn't. Where I failed myself was that I desperately desired acceptance, love and respect and fooled myself into thinking that I could somehow get it from somebody who wasn't capable of even loving himself.

Chapter 3

"Positive anything is better than negative nothing."

~Elbert Hubbard

There are so many people who ask me today how I was stuck for so long, and why did I go back in the past after attempting several times of getting away. The funny thing about people is how they try to understand something they haven't really lived through themselves. They begin to opinionate and even impose their beliefs on you and speak them over you. Unfortunately, people want to believe that they have the answers and will often meddle in ways that are neither helpful nor productive. For example; it took me 21 years to finally be completely free of a very bad relationship - from the outside of my situation looking in, a lot of people really had no idea what I was going through. They could speculate or assume to know but the truth is that unless you are living through it, you don't really know what is occurring behind those closed doors and how the people involved feel.

If you are trying to help somebody who is in a situation they are trying to get out of, please do not continually ask them why they stayed so long and why they went back in the past. What you are actually doing is hurting them by making them feel like they have failed. In a sense, this is victim shaming and nobody has any right to make anyone feel bad for something they probably have no control over at that time. Unless your words are encouraging, keep it to yourself. You are doing more damage than you think.

Nothing made me feel worse than to repeatedly explain why I felt stuck and why I failed at previous attempts to leave. On top of that; I was struggling with the guilt within myself because we had other children after the loss of that first baby. At the beginning, I mention that my parents had been divorced and I didn't want to put my own children through that similar pain. When there are children involved, the last thing any parent wants to do is harm his or her children. Where I fell short as a mother was that it took me time to recognize that it was actually more harmful to the children by staying.

Depression in full swing is a massive crippler. The shadow of darkness which blankets you can ultimately blind you and cause you to lose your self.

I was only 16 when I began the relationship; I can honestly tell you that I went from childhood to being an adult without reasonable time to even grow into my own. I've never had the opportunity to know what it was like to go to a senior prom. I continued to have children, yet I had no idea how good it felt to just have a day with friends to hangout and talk and be social. In fact I never had that before the relationship so it's safe to say that I never really got to live in a healthy and productive way.

There are days that I listen to people talk about their memories and it makes me want to cry. I hear the joy and happiness in their voices as they discuss these things that I never had the freedom to experience. The social awkwardness went from moderate to extreme so making any friends during the relationship was deemed impossible. It was only when he wasn't around that I'd try to fit in and enjoy the company of other people. To this day, I maintain that my best adult memories stem from being at work because the only freedom I had to be myself was within those 8 hours.

If you begin to see that you too are feeling the same way, then you have to step back and really evaluate your situation. As an individual, we should have the time to be ourselves without worrying if we're going to do something wrong somehow to our significant other. When you feel like everything you do may be seen as some sort of mistake, then you are literally trapped in a sticky web while getting the life sucked out of you.

Being caught in this web can really kill your soul and that is how it has always felt to me. I developed a deep and incurable emptiness that couldn't be filled as a result of too much being taken away. The guilt that was bestowed upon me was so thick that I felt like I was drowning. If I so much as smiled at a person of the opposite sex, I was belittled, accused, embarrassed in public and screamed at. In no way whatsoever does anyone have the right to do this to another person. People are naturally social creatures and we need more interaction than just the people living with us. All this did was make me feel like if I even attempted to have any sort of friendship, I would be kicked down and ripped apart - this made me afraid of other people. I would be in so much pain inside of myself if anyone paid attention to me that it reached a point where all I wanted to do was stay home and hide.

The amount of depression which follows this is immeasurable. Once I began to feel hopeless, it was coupled with feeling completely alone and isolated from the world. It is within this crippling mindset that they attain their power over you because now they're in total control and why should that ever be allowed? The one constant thought that I had a hard time with was the belief that the world had forgotten me and I was alone in this and somehow deserved it. Since being out of the situation, I have come to realize that more and more people were quite aware and not only that, I discovered that many of them could actually relate.

One of the continual problems I faced was the inability to see a way out. For the longest time I nearly believed that these things in which I was living through were indeed normal and I just assumed other relationships were carried out the same way.

As I tried to seclude myself within my own mind, I would get a glimpse of what a real loving relationship truly looked like through my parents and others. The problem was that I had been torn down so bad that I was convinced that I wasn't personally good enough or capable enough to be loved and appreciated and treated the way others were. I had come to believe that all I did was make these constant mistakes and he'd make me think *who could love somebody like that? Someone who was constantly torn down, spit at, belittled, shoved back and a constant recipient of verbal hate.*

To think like that is a rather severe self-destructive act I had done to myself; by doing this, I enabled him to carry on controlling me because I was led to believe through his actions that I am simply not worthy of anything better and nobody else would ever want me.

In hindsight; I think about my inner thoughts quite often and I can see how I held myself back. There was so much time that I wasted to negative thoughts and selflessness and I disabled myself from actually seeing the truth. When you begin to hate yourself and reject who you are, it's about as equal to being a drone - a brainwashed shell of an existence just going through the motions of life with disregard for your self ... but I know now that I am better than that. And so are you.

To use an example: If something had gone wrong with a vehicle we were driving, it was automatically my fault. I had somehow in some way caused the vehicle to break down and the blame would escalate to a level where I was made to feel worthless. That literal thought is still with me at times today. As I write this book, I am still healing and it may take a while before I have completely set those feelings free but in no way should I have ever let myself believe that it was okay to sit there and allow this person to kick me down for every single thing that had gone wrong. If there is one thing anyone reading this book can learn from my experience; I want you to really understand that not everything is your fault if at all and there is absolutely nothing wrong with you. If they love you they complement you, and they merely fix whatever problem has occurred and they certainly wouldn't ever shame you or belittle you for simple mechanical errors.

Have you ever been blamed for something that somebody else has said or done? I can't think of anything that is more confusing than being torn down for something that another person said or did. When this happened to me, I eventually began to say in response "man I must be a powerful and magical person to be able to control the actions of another" and that is how ridiculous it really is. If he hits you, you didn't ask for it. If someone spoke up because they noticed something, you didn't cause that ... there is something called free will! We have to be empowered by knowing that we are not the problem when someone else is taking something out on us. What I have come to learn from my own experiences is that the problem is actually within them. For whatever reason, there is something they can't contain or control whether it's their own guilt or perhaps deeper problems that we aren't aware of. I lost count on how many times I have heard somebody tell me that a person cheating will accuse their lover of the very act when they are guilty themselves. It also amazes me how many people have talked with me about being hit or torn down mentally while being accused of such. They act out like this because they are trying to hide their own guilt. Never allow yourself to accept the responsibility of something that you have no control over, you do not deserve it.

It took me a very long time to really understand that for myself and I realize it make take some of you a very long time. Think about your life before the situation. Think about your happiness and who you were. Did you lose any of that? Was there a point in the time with the person you are with now where you felt like everything you did was wrong? How about before that?

In my relationship with the abuser, I felt dehumanized to the point that I wasn't a person any longer. I had become an object of sorts in which I believed at the time that this was all that I was worth. That horrid sense of selflessness in one of the biggest cripplers if you allow it to become. You have to understand that you do have the power to prevent that from happening to you, and that you do not deserve to feel that way.

When we are born, we are free and limitless. We grow and become into our own and our personalities develop while we grow and learn. During your adolescence, you learn how to abide by rules because children have no way of knowing right from wrong unless it is taught to them. An example: Tommy is told that it is not okay to hit Sally because it is not okay to hit girls for whatever reason. Tommy is also told that he should not hit Jack because hitting anyone isn't acceptable behavior and this will land him in detention. Therefore, Tommy learns that there will be repercussions for his actions if he hits either Sally or Jack. This is obviously a rather mundane and simple example but a very important one that I want you to keep in mind.

We grow into young adults now having learned the basic rules of life (what we should or should not do) and in all of those lessons, you should have understood that though society does have rules, you are a free soul who is able to make your own decisions and choices and you are aware that bad behavior has its repercussions. If you steal from the store you might end up in jail. If you show an act of kindness to a person in need, you will probably be rewarded in one way or another. Some rewards are feeling better about ourselves because we put somebody else's needs first. If you choose to be a rotten person to others, there are also circumstances that you may deal with such as guilt and bitterness. It is you who is in control of yourself and it is you who has the decision of what is good or bad for you. In no way whatsoever should we be made to feel like we must give up the power over ourselves to anyone for they do not deserve that right no matter what they say or do to us.

I know how hard that may be to understand. When I was in my former relationship, I was made to feel guilty for many things that I really shouldn't have felt guilt about at all. One of the things I felt the most guilt from was trying to have friendships. Because we had children together, he convinced me that he had the right to come and go as he desired while I stayed home constantly with children.

Being a mother was certainly an amazing gift bestowed upon me, but without ever having time to be myself, it also took a serious toll. My older children are angry with me today and they are still living with him. It should come as no surprise that the abusers will turn your own kids against you by using such claims as "she abandoned us" because it's easy for them to employ. I did have to overcome some personal guilt to make the steps it took to change my situation. A lot of women in my similar situation also made mention of their children and why they wouldn't make the steps to change the bad situation. I can respect this and I do understand because I have sacrificed for my own children but when is it enough, and why would it be healthy to stay?

Whatever you are going through in your home, you have to acknowledge that your children are also susceptible to the situations.

For the longest time I had convinced myself that I wouldn't put my own kids through the separation of their parents but in those years, they had also suffered mentally and emotionally along side me. Not only was it hard for them because of the constant arguments; there were periods where I'd also react badly myself. I will never pretend that I was a perfect parent by any means, but really ... who is? I was enduring so much negativity myself that it would spill out onto my kids and anyone that was around me. I would catch myself acting out sometimes and I would get real upset about it later. There was this enormous cloud of depression and hopelessness that draped over me so it had become hard to contain myself while in extreme moments of stress or anxiety.

Happiness has to first start at home. When you wake up, you shouldn't be made to feel like once you sit up and get ready for your day that for whatever reason some sort of anger will be spilled out onto you, and in my case that happened daily. Eventually I began to dread waking up before him and it reached a point where I'd simply desire to stay in bed until it seemed safe enough to get up. This also can catch up to you and cause you some really unkind inner thoughts. Even today, when I first wake up, I kind of lie there because I had become so used to that behavior until something within myself says "Hey it's okay, now get up." Idle activity is the body's biggest enemy. When you begin to train yourself into such inactivity, you are choosing to accept a decline in physical health. We have to move for our blood to flow because the body needs to remain active. With proper blood flow, you begin to have more energy and with more energy you are more productive and being productive can reduce our risk of being suspended in depression. I encourage you to remember your own health as it is just as important as our children. When we are in poor health we do not care and if we don't care we don't try and if we don't try we let them win. Do you really want to give in and hand someone the key to *your* life?

As of so far, I hope you are beginning to see that a lot of their power is given to them from us and that you want to be in control of yourself.

Mental programming isn't just something you'd expect to read about in a science fiction novel or see in a futuristic movie. Mental programming is where someone persistently works on convincing you of specific thoughts such as not being worthy, or good enough and this abuse can be worse than physical abuse. How many times have you heard someone complain about being punched some ten or twenty years ago? Physical altercations are undoubtedly uncalled for. In no situation ever should anyone be hit, kicked, or bit and nothing really justifies that behavior, but let's be real here, it does happen and it does hurt during the time but the pain goes away. If anything, we look back and think about how we felt at the time and in some cases, even laugh it off and move on.

"Sticks and stones may break my bones, but names will never hurt me." We have all recited this rhyme in our youth or heard it at one time or another. The truth is that we have feelings and we have thoughts about those names and other words of anger. I have had the physical altercations but I must however confess that the verbal, mental and emotional attacks hurt much worse. There is no magical band-aid to take away the scars that words can leave inside - I went through some therapy myself and it did help but despite those efforts, a lot of that stayed with me for a very long time and that is what mental programming actually is. It's years of systematic and persistent suggestion that I wasn't good enough, that I was second or even third best, that I wasn't smart ... the list goes on and on. Am I really a slut? A whore? Worthless? Useless? Retarded? Ugly?

Nothing gives anyone the right to say a single judgmental or bad word about you. I want you to ask yourself this right now! Where do they actually have this right to demean you and cut you down and belittle you to the point of feeling so inferior that you'd rather be dead than wake up? God forbid you make a mistake, it only means that if you didn't do something his way that you are certain to be screamed at like a dog who just shat all over the entire house while dragging the garbage around the recently scrubbed kitchen floor. Hey, I have some good news for you reading this; you are none of those ugly names nor mistakes he may want you to believe you are and I really want you to acknowledge that. I want you to look into a mirror and really *see* yourself. I want you to see how beautiful you are, and how strong you are because hey, you're still breathing baby and in time you'll gain the strength to walk out of that door and say enough is enough!

I know that you want to tell me that it's easier said than done, and what do I know? You need to know that I was you ... For 21 years I was exactly where you are now and I thought exactly the same way. Flirting with the idea of breaking free from such a situation can even seem completely overwhelming at first but you need to realize that you mustn't give in to self doubt or even for a matter of temporary convenience.

I wasn't allowed to obtain and/or maintain employment which meant I was faced with the thought of *how will I ever be free from this hell?* The obstacle with abusive relationships is the isolation from the world because that's what they want to achieve; they want to prevent you from your own independence because they are aware that if you are strong enough to stand on your own two feet, you are capable enough of finding a way out. In some situations, you may not be able to get an opportunity to ever obtain a job and this may render you utterly hopeless. Nobody wants to leave a fully furnished home and relocate to the streets. Too often there exist these situations where the abused woman has a fully furnished home complete with everything she may need and so she will settle because she is provided for in a material sense. What she is really doing is putting herself aside for the necessities that are provided to her for an artificial sense of comfort.

There were things I was provided such as satellite television, a modern, computer, cell phone, washer & dryer, a roof over my head and food. The importance of those things are rather insignificant if you compare it to the situation I was living with daily. Though I had the computer, I was shamed for using it. Though I had a cell phone, I was belittled and cursed for using it. Though I had the large variety of channels to choose from, I was made to feel guilty for ever having a desire to watch something that interested me. Though simple luxuries did exist, I was constantly defending myself for choosing to use them. How is that living? I ask myself this very question even now; how could I have ever settled for such a death sentence? Though I am still alive and well, I was brought down so bad by him that it literally did feel like I was slowly dying.

Is it *really* worth it?

Chapter 4

"Yesterday is not ours to recover,
but tomorrow is ours to win or lose."

~ Lyndon B. Johnson

One of the most ignored circumstances (at least in my own experiences) is the mental decline while living in an abusive relationship. As I have already mentioned, there is massive amounts of depression from the isolation and this renders the lack of self confidence. Without any self confidence, I was led on a direct path to suicidal thoughts. In this chapter, I am going to talk a lot about my own personal mindset and what eventually helped me to see beyond the dark shroud that blocked my vision.

One of my lifelong gifts is a creative imagination and the ability to write. Before I undertook the task of this novel, I had witnessed the success of my short story *'What has Kenneth Done!'* and various choice romantic-era language poetry see distributable publication. It was an indescribable joy to witness something that I put my mind to reach a level of success that went beyond sitting in some blog someplace. Indeed, it didn't go viral and it may not impress all readers, but it was deemed worthy enough to be published in a collection of short stories along-side some really gifted authors. I had also worked my way up in a society in which worked within the scientific field for paranormal research to the point of making senior director. "What does this have to do with abuse?" you might be asking yourself. I reached these successes while still in that relationship. Despite the name-calling and endless let-downs and years upon years of crippling depression, I somehow pushed through it and gained some much needed confidence.

The first five years of my abusive relationship, I was either pregnant or struggling to survive with the post-traumatic depression. There was a burning desire deep within that really wanted to come out and persevere. In one extreme, I was constantly kicked down and called such names as retarded, or stupid and this planted enough seeds within my mind to grow and manifest itself into actual personal beliefs. In another extreme, the person who I used to be was screaming her head off and saying "stand up god damn it and show them what you really are!"

Any victim turned survivor coming out of whatever situation they made it through will tell you that something inside of them ignored the fables of negative thoughts and it pushed them to stand up and fight for themselves.

As the years began to build and pile up on top of me, I did begin to lose any rational sense of hope. I had already tried on numerous occasions to leave the abusive relationship. During each failed attempt, he was right there saying how sorry he was and how much he loved me and that things will be different this time. After the third time, nothing was changing and it was in fact getting worse. So here I was with children in common deceivingly sacrificing from myself for them. I would let the kids become the sole reason why I'd go back.

The help was there, but I couldn't then see it. On my third attempt, I had actually gone to my mother and I was trying to stabilize myself enough to get on my own feet and provide for them. Because I had been told so often how useless and worthless I was, my self-confidence was right out the window. There was nothing I wanted more than to succeed at breaking free with the ability to care for the kids independently but despite my efforts, I lost any motivation to even try.

Now I was faced with the sobering reality (or so I thought at the time) that I may never be able to break free from him and the relationship. Not only was I in a prison he designed, but I was also locked into one that my own mind designed. We can be completely blind and place the entire blame on the abuser, or we can accept that we are also to blame. Maybe that seems incredible for me to say to you, or maybe you completely agree and understand that you do have the choice over your own life and who you choose to be in it. Did the abusive situation set up the mental programming? Absolutely.

To prove my point, I want you to do a little science experiment. I want you to take two jars and fill them both with white rice. After you have done this, name both of the jars whatever feels right to you and choose between the two of them which one you will speak love over, and which one you will speak hate over. Do this for about a week: the jar you choose to speak hate over, begin telling it how awful and despicable it is. Tell it how you hate it and hope it dies and how it isn't good enough. The jar you choose to speak love over, begin telling it how beautiful and wonderful it is and how much you love it. I have done this very experiment myself; after about a week, the jar of love still looked incredibly healthy whereas the jar of hate began to discolor and look rotten. Now, envision yourself as the jars of rice. What is happening to you with the negative words being spoken over you? You are not going to be the beautiful and incredible person that you are meant to be. Your inner person will become as rotten and discolored as the rice.

The mental programming will rot you inside much like the experiment. By acknowledging this, you must also acknowledge that you have to somehow step out of negativity before you can begin to heal. There has to be something that gives you joy whether it is writing, painting, photography, walking, or perhaps your own children. Find that positive in your surroundings and begin to build back that confidence you have long since lost much like I had with writing. No matter how big or how small, just the accomplishment will deliver you with the much needed positive mindset that you need to focus on.

Acceptance of anything positive may take you a lot of time but you will be rewarded at each successful attempt.

Within the numerous failed attempts of escaping, this built a conundrum of tunneled thoughts that walked me right into the belief that death was the only option available to me. It is indeed overwhelmingly crippling when you begin to take this thought very seriously. I recall sitting still for hours in deep calculating thought of how I would achieve death and why it would become a practical choice for breaking free. What I was doing was convincing myself.

As each morning came and I saw my children, I would struggle with this thought process. I would begin to think about how it would effect them and I tried to ignore the persistence of those thoughts. However; these thoughts were so constant that I couldn't completely shut them out. It wasn't long before the hopelessness overtook logic.

When you become consumed with this type of thinking, anything else just seems to fade away. At any point, I could have reached out and sought help but unfortunately I was already lost to the hopeless mindset and without any idea of knowing where to reach out. There was no support available to me. We did have the internet; I knew that whatever I was looking into would somehow be found out and the last thing I wanted to do was to anger him any further than he already was. There would be days where we had to go fill out paperwork for county services and on the walls I would notice the posters for such organizations as Victims Of Violence. He was constantly watching my every move and I was never able to grab a pamphlet but luckily they displayed their phone number right on the face of the poster. I would repeat the number in my mind as a way of memorizing it. The next step would be to have that moment to actually dial the number if should an opportunity became available. During this period of my life, we didn't have a home phone and there was no cell phone nor a neighbor I could go to. What I really should have done was found the confidence to take the risk in trusting one of the neighbors enough to make the call. In no way should I have ever convinced myself that everyone is 'on his side' because when I did that, I was literally handing him a power he didn't deserve. I allowed myself to believe that if the neighbor listened to me, he or she would say something to him - in this instance, I built my own prison walls even stronger by allowing myself to believe that I will never escape.

With an ever deeper sense of hopelessness sinking in, I began to obsess over various methods of how I would complete a successful suicide attempt. As I thought through the various ways to achieve it, each time I would consider my children and realize that in no way would I ever want them to discover my lifeless body. Although I was suffering so deeply, I had always kept their best interests a priority high above myself. However; despite the satisfaction of children and the love that we share and receive from them, there comes a time where the pain surpasses.

Now I had numerous angles of pain; physical from a job where I was prepping food and lifting 25 to 50 pounds at a time, and mental from my home situation of continued name-calling and constant verbal disputes. For a (then) 23 year-old, I felt like I was much older. Where the work environment offered me a sense of peace being away from him; it was a rather busy restaurant inside of a thruway rest stop at a high-demand location. The thought of calling the Victims of Violence number from work was there, but I prevented myself from making the call by convincing myself that it was simply 'too busy' and that there was no time. The truth was that I had breaks and I could have called during those breaks, but my mind (at that time) kind of worked against me. The fear of the 'what ifs' or 'he will find out' tore me away from ever taking the chance.

In numerous failed attempts to alleviate the lower back pain from the heavy lifting, I was introduced to the painkiller known as *Oxycontin* through one of his family members. Remember, I was already deep in suicidal thoughts due to the ongoing belief that I had no way out as well as dealing daily with the continued verbal insults that only subsided when he wasn't home. I also had 3 young children that I was trying to raise without any help or relief. He would come and go as he pleased while I was left to tend to the children and if I had to go anywhere, they were to always go with me. Just imagine: I was working a physically straining job where one night I'd close only to return the next morning to open on a 36 to 40 hour a week work schedule. Add to that a 6 year old, a 5 year old and a 3 year old child who need constant attention on top of house duties such as cooking, cleaning and laundry. He was rarely, if ever home to assist and the times that he was, he wasn't a real big help and only chose to cut me down verbally while nothing I did was ever good enough. With all of that responsibility and never a moment's break, I didn't even have enough time to breathe a sigh of relief. The introduction to the painkiller now became my only avenue to any escape of the stress and pain.

Before I realized it; I had become helplessly addicted to the feeling received through some various painkillers such as the Oxycontin, Hydrocodone, and whatever else I could get my hands on. Do not misunderstand me; I was in pain, and desperately alone and filled with fear. By using the pain medication, I was destructively making a wrong choice. The so-called relief was short term, and if anything, misinterpreted as some sort of escape from reality. However; like anything else which is used as a method of escape, it renders very sad and temporary results that leave you in a cocoon of nothingness and tormenting withdrawal.

It wasn't long before I could identify with the inability to truly relieve the pain and recognize that I was only addicted to a chemical of a false and temporary happiness. This newfound addiction went on for about a year and that is when my mind entwined the suicidal thoughts together with the idea that the painkillers may only alleviate pain for hours but with enough of them, perhaps I could reach my goal of escape through death.

Carefully, I began to assess how much of which pill if mixed with another would ultimately work to achieve a death by overdose. I was truly convinced that I would reach this goal and took no precautions to get away from him. From there, I disappeared into the night to find a motel room far enough away where I could commence ingesting the medication and fall asleep for the last time without interference. My certainty was so profound that I didn't hesitate swallowing the pills once I was settled in the room. It wasn't just one, or two, or even three; with a 20 oz. bottle of Mountain Dew, I swallowed at least 40 painkillers (which was a mix of two different kinds) and then laid in the center of the bed. It wasn't long before I could feel the effects set in, and not much longer thereafter when I felt myself slip away.

If you've ever heard an NDE (Near Death Experience) story; most people talk about seeing a light and experiencing feelings of unexplainable comfort and freedom. This was mostly true for me; however, I first saw a wall of darkness. It felt empty and a little incomplete - there was a sense of freedom but just as the darkness gave way, I began to witness my own life review.

A life review is where you see a rerun of all the happiest moments of your life play out in front of you while you're slipping away.

The faces of the people I loved the most flashed before my eyes. First I saw the faces of my children, and the day each one of them were born. The moments of happiness I experienced with them flashed by my eyes in a fashion similar to putting a VCR on the fast-forward motion. After; I saw my parents and my brother as well as the day when I was outside at the age of 5 by myself in an enormous grassy field and I was surrounded by butterflies. There beside me looking up was a baby; my baby that I had lost in 1994 and she just smiled at me. When I smiled back, my great-grandmother appeared before me and said "Your journey hasn't even begun, you must go back." and just like that, I woke up with a burning sensation in my chest and a heavy state of vertigo. I managed to roll to the floor and I fought myself to remain conscious as I made my way into the bathroom to disgorge the contents in my stomach.

If anything; what I took from that desperate and rock-bottom moment of my life was that in order to really live, I had to first die.

This meant that I had to kick away the addiction, and walk away from the suicidal approach; like all things we struggle to release from ourselves, this too would prove to be a much larger obstacle piled on top of the situation that I was already stuck in.

There's no doubt in my mind that some of you reading my story may have thought about suicide as a way of escape. Perhaps you may not want to admit it to anyone, or even yourself but I want you to really think about this. You need to really think about *who* you would really be hurting if you were to succeed. You may want to believe that it's some sort of ultimate payback to your abuser or that it is the only way to truly be free from the situation - do not fool yourself into that type of thinking, there are other ways out and all you have to do is to become brave enough and educate yourself whenever there's an opportunity.

Choosing suicide as my way out was not only selfish, but incredibly foolish. My children would have to grow up without their mother and my parents would have grieved and possibly blamed themselves for something that wasn't their fault. I would have never experienced adult life with a certain level of freedom I have since attained. My other two children would have never been born. I would have never fallen in real love and met my soul mate. But worst of all; the abuser would have won. Think about that long and hard ... Suicide does not set you free, it disperses pain onto those who truly loved you and rips you out of their lives forever. They will have to try and live the rest of their lives wondering what they could have done to help you—do you think that's what you really want and is that really fair to them?

As I laid in that room after emptying my stomach contents; in my weakened and troubled state, all I could think of was how guilty I had felt for attempting to end my life. A large part of myself really wanted to turn back the clock to the day I chose to accept the narcotic pill. The person who handed me the pill didn't put a gun to my head and force me to take it. I chose to ingest that pill and the numerous thereafter. It was me who decided to hang on tightly to a terrible addiction as a desperate way to escape the reality that I was living in. What saved me was the acceptance of my own mistakes and taking the responsibility for my own choices. At any moment, I could have easily blamed my situation on someone else, and I could have blamed my parents for not helping, or anyone else who knew what was going on. In truth, the blame was on me. Surviving my suicidal attempt transformed me. That was the very moment that I was no longer a victim and I had transformed into a survivor.

I knew that I had to kick that drug addiction. Some people explain that overcoming an addiction was extremely hard for them but I have to be honest and tell you that after the first week, I was free from the hold that it had on me. It was conquering that demon which helped me to realize that I could do anything if I just put my mind to it. The symptoms of withdrawal would come and go; I slept through a great deal of it and focused on ideas for writing.

Once upon a time within the vast and growing monster known as the world wide web, I discovered myself by way of micro-blogging. There was a time when I placed a high importance on the use of this as a way develop my writing ability. Perhaps my sub-conscious understood that this tool made available to me would help me grow as an individual in a way that I wasn't allowed to otherwise. My sub-conscious also recognized that I needed to direct all of my focus on constantly creating new ideas as opposed to the painful situation. In a way, I can admit that it grew into another escape from my reality because it allowed me to express myself anonymously in a creative community - here existed a collection of creative people, and other like-minds of whom I could invisibly hold conversations with in the form of e-mails and other text. That freedom to have these adult friends; people he had no way of chasing away was an awakening and empowering revelation in my life.

Now I had found a little freedom to grow into who I was meant to be without any type of fear holding me back. As much as I detest a lot of social media; what that diary website really gave me was the ability to freely mature without restriction and become who I was meant to be without anyone else controlling the direction I needed to take for myself.

Chapter 5

At the beginning of chapter 4 I mentioned my gained successes in writing; we will now go over the importance of those successes as it relates to my struggles, and eventual freedom.

In a toxic relationship; you as the recipient will begin to feel unworthy of anything and will even believe that you aren't good enough or able enough to succeed. In my case, he had repeatedly referred to me as 'stupid' 'retarded' ignorant' and 'unable to do anything right.' Because he had so often repeated this to me, I began to believe these untrue statements and found myself unable to believe otherwise.

There still existed something within myself which reminded me that I do have some incredible talents and that I should give those talents a real chance as opposed to setting it aside. As I researched outlets on the internet, I came across a website that hosted online diaries. While initially looking at it I remember thinking that the concept of putting our secret thoughts out there for the public was a truly ridiculous idea. Some of the titles of people's entries were displayed on the right hand side, and below the title was the beginning contents. I immediately realized that people weren't using this site as a diary at all, but rather a public place to share their creative writing. I took the plunge and created my own little section within the site and almost immediately began formulating ideas for short poems and stories.

It wasn't long before the positive notes of encouragement began flowing in. As I would read each comment of praise and even bits of creative criticism, it was then that I found the very tool to build back my self confidence.

The interaction alone was a wonderful breath of fresh air. Here are people actually suggesting to me that something in which I had originally created was brilliant; not stupid, or retarded, or worthless, but brilliant. This was exactly what I needed to begin overcoming those years where the abuser was trying to tell me otherwise. The internet, no matter how many negative stories we may hear about it had now given me that glimpse of light I had so long searched for. Someone outside of my own parents had now told me that I have the ability to really succeed if I would only try.

When our parents encourage us, it is to be expected. They love us, they raise us, and send us out into the world while praising us and of course it feels good to hear your mother or father support you in those ways. When people who have no relationship or connection to you begin to praise you, that is when it begins to feel real and truly deserving. It shows that your efforts have paid off in a way that rewards your personal self esteem each time a new and unrelated person expresses something positive about you or your work.

With my newfound confidence; I continued to develop my writing abilities and work at ways for improving my works. Not too long after this wonderful blessing he discovered that I was spending time working at my writing - he immediately found ways to belittle me and of course anything that I was doing as a way to discourage me from it altogether.

It first started with little comments about spending too much time on a computer. He found any and every excuse to tell me why I am a bad person and doing bad things. From there he turned it into something it wasn't by suggesting I was only talking to men and how this makes me a whore and a pig. Of course I was exchanging messages with people but what he didn't realize and couldn't conceive was that what was really happening were exchanges of praise and support from other aspiring authors. He tried to take this very positive activity away from me by making it into something else entirely. He was now beginning to realize that I could and was able to reach the outside world and that endangered the walls of his well-built prison. He also realized that not only did I have the confidence to continually do it, but that his fears of my strengths to overcome his hold on me will eventually become a reality.

He'd begin to threaten to take the internet modem out of the house. Frightened of what would happen to me, I stood up to him and threatened to leave if he ever removed the equipment. At that time, I realistically had nowhere I could have gone to but I was desperate not to lose my only window into the world outside of that damn house.

My strength in standing up against him about something so minor also began to empower me into seeing that with a bit more confidence, I could and would be able to eventually lock down a way to get free.

My very first step in conceiving a safe way was to be realistic. With now 4 children; an escape and practical means would obviously take money. By this point however, I had lost the full-time restaurant job after being made to feel guilty about leaving the home to work. His jabs and other menacing comments towards my leaving to make minimum wage had led me to feel a horrible sense of guilt about leaving my children while trying to earn money. What occurred to me shortly thereafter losing that particular job was that I was gulled into thinking that I was doing a great injustice to the family when really I was bringing in enough money to pay bills and supply food.

His answer for the food situation then and remained continually through the whole relationship was that I was harming the family for the added income because they would lower the amount of food stamp benefits that he was receiving. He didn't see the change in benefits as a way to eventually crawl out of poverty but rather viewed it as a crippler to confine me and discourage me from any sort of occupation that would lower the monthly amount that he would receive.

Upon this realization, I began to scour the internet for a new job that would pay a little better than minimum wage as I began to teach myself new writing methods. It was through a series of literature books that his cousin had given me that I discovered the unique writing techniques of such authors as William Shakespeare and Oscar Wilde. From there I continued to discover other authors who varied in style and composition - I would practice the exercises after understanding the lessons which were offered in those books. At each attempt to understand the lessons, I gained much more confidence while replacing a bit of my self-esteem. All of those circulating thoughts that I once had of *I can't* and *I am not worthy* and *I am not good enough* began to disappear. Not only was I educating myself with the literature, I was as well rebuilding the fragments of confidence I had long ago lost.

The power that I began to feel from successfully understanding that I am capable of much greater things was now positioning me into actually believing that I can and will become free from the life he had me trapped in. Now it had become a real possibility that not only would I be able to get out and take care of myself, but that I wasn't any of the things he wanted me to believe of myself and I was not as ignorant as he would have liked me to believe.

Those long and lonely nights of second guessing my own intelligence, and trying to reason with the circling thoughts of being the person who could never do a thing right were beginning to disappear. That shroud that he wanted placed over my eyes was turning transparent and there wasn't a thing he could do about it. I may not have had a job or the means to get away just then; I did however have the tools within my mind to know despite the fear and the struggles and the negative thoughts, I was able to overcome it.

He began to really see that he was losing a bit of that control and would work extra hard at convincing me of what a foolish failure and shame I was to him. He first did this by defaming me to others to give off this sense that I was obviously mentally ill. His means of convincing them was to suggest that I was delusional and obsessive. At the very beginning of that, it really bothered me that I was being labeled and judged unfairly. He would suggest that I was either bipolar or manic in some fashion. Really, he tried suggesting anything to make me appear as though I was off my rocker although he wouldn't hesitate to never be home to assist with raising the children. If nobody could see that he was suggesting I was crazy and yet he often left home leaving me responsible for the children, then it occurred to me that their opinion was about as useful as a fart in a jar.

Instead of letting this stunt of his knock me off track; I looked for ways to actually use it to my advantage. While he was present, I gave him exactly what he called me; the illusion of being off my rocker. This ridiculous diversion would direct his attention away from what I was really doing and assist me to discovering ways and seeking out jobs that would enable me to escape.

My only issue at that point wasn't what he or his family thought of me, but the fact that I had a terrible work history. His constant attempts to disable my progress were damaging through the relationship, I was never able to keep a job very long - I was lucky to even have transport to the place of employment let alone the ability to get out of the door and make it to work.

On one occasion; I was out in the driveway preparing to leave when he had become so upset that he tried to actually pin me by the legs between my car and his truck. Luckily I was able to jump out of the way in just enough time to avoid being crushed. Had I not been paying attention to what he was doing, I would have been badly injured. In an ironic turn of events, he of course later apologized and tried to convince me that he loved me and was sorry and how it wouldn't ever happen again. He went on to suggest it was my fault because he felt like I was in a hurry to meet someone at work (as though I even had the time to do anything like that.) On that same day, I did actually leave work early to go stay with my brother in his apartment. This didn't pan out for me because he was still in possession of the kids and I couldn't bring myself to leave them behind. I also couldn't bring them to my brother's apartment and expect him to allow all of us to stay with him as he was barely supporting his self while attending college. That escape was a last-minute, and very poorly planned dash into the night.

However badly planned, that failed attempt did not for a moment discourage me from the hope that one day I will be able to break free. If anything, it became a lesson of what not to do in future attempts.

The first month after returning from that specific escape, he produced the facade of changing for the better and no matter how much he tried, I wasn't convinced. This was the pivotal point where I can describe it as sleeping with the enemy. His days of fooling me or coercing me were long gone and despite anything he said or did, there was no doubt that I knew better. By truly seeing the beast for what it is, there is a certain amount of power you begin to absorb. This is the point where you know damn well he will lie to you and do or say anything to persuade you and all of it is meaningless and fictitious. You would be further ahead picking up a novel because anything is more believable than the nonsense you're being fed by a man who doesn't even realize that you're smart to his bullshit.

When you have reached this point, you will begin to look back, and those memories are going to come in hard and fast. You are going to lie there and watch those long and painful nights play out over and over again. A big part of you may want to scream in anger and maybe you ought to. Let yourself get angry! Let go and really let it come out because you have got to begin releasing it from your soul. Embrace those emotions and begin to tell yourself that you do not want to live this way anymore. Remind yourself that there is an entire world outside of that house and there are people that exist in it who will really love you and see your worth. As that anger escapes and the tears finally dry up, repeat this to yourself: *I am better than this. I do not deserve to be hit. I will not let him put me down anymore. I will not give up.* Most importantly; *I will get out!*

With a composition book and a pen, I began to write those statements in repetition. After all, he used repetitious attacks to convince me otherwise, so I used the same exact tactic to tell myself that I will get out, I will not give up, and that I am better than this. By hearing yourself saying those verses and seeing the words before you on paper, you are literally building yourself up. Your mind will begin to accept these positives over the negative programming that you were previously susceptible to. It is also a step forward in your own self-esteem. You have to remember to love yourself and see that you do matter. When you have low or no self-esteem, that is when you are more susceptible to the negative beliefs. They work hard to kick us down by calling us everything from useless to fat, or ugly, or worthless, useless, meaningless, and they even convince you that nobody cares about you.

I spent most of my life believing things about myself such as being worthless, ugly, fat, unwanted, unlovable, and incapable. There was a period of time where I even began to believe I really was insane and paranoid when neither was the case. He had worked so hard at convincing me with repetitive reminders that I couldn't believe anything different.

The original momentum from the online diary deserves all the credit in the world for saving me from myself. That web presence gave me more courage and love and strength than anything before it in my life. Strangers revealed this whole other side of life to me that I never before knew. I discovered that genuine and honest people do exist out there who want nothing more in return than simple friendship. It also showed me that deep within myself exists the real me who was tired of being kicked down and shoved in the corner like a trophy.

My success at publication was eventual. I now had the knowledge and tools to establish myself as well as the courage to follow through with it. My supporting words to myself from my first draft to finished product was and still is *never give up.* When I felt like I was about to ditch the project, I would go back to write down, read, and reread those three simple words. Never give up.

Chapter 6

"Desperation is the raw material of drastic change.
Only those who can leave behind everything
they have ever believed in can hope to escape."

~ William S. Burroughs

With newfound strength comes the ability to change the situation but even in our complete confidence, we can and will become desperate.

I wanted it so bad and so immediate. The chance that I could finally break free was such an intense realization that I grabbed on to it and began desperately seeking an opportunity to run fast and far. The impulsiveness of knowing I can and am able to go through with leaving sort of dampened any level of common sense. What I lacked was a plan and any sense of focus. The power of determination can sometimes render you blind to the bigger picture because all you can see are the intended rewards.

Sometimes blindness can also corrupt your sense of better judgment. In my case; a neighbor and his family had known of the ongoing battles I was living through and actually offered a helping hand. What I didn't know was that they possessed a motive of their own. My first mistake was not taking the time to ask myself why they were so forthcoming and persistent with removing me from the bad situation.

One of the things you must remember is that sometimes you will cross others in life who will take advantage of an already bad situation to make a profit of their own. When something comes along that holds out a helping hand yet your gut instinct is not to trust it, then take note of your instinct. You are going to become desperate, impulsive, blind, and in that adrenaline fueled rush of fear I can guarantee you that you are going to make some serious mistakes.

You have to recognize the difference between genuine help versus ulterior motives. I do not want to dissuade you from reaching out; there are people out there who can and will help you when you realize that it is time to break away.

The neighbor who wanted to help me actually didn't care about my situation at all; rather, he wanted a free pass into the house as a way to gain possession of property in order to resell it or barter with it. For him, it was a way to take advantage of an otherwise delicate situation for his own selfish needs. In order to gain my trust, he and his wife offered to let me use one of their vehicles since my abuser took it upon himself to take mine away from me. The abuser was smart on placing the titles of the motor vehicles in his name so that I would never have a right to my own transportation.

Because of a physical altercation between the abuser and myself; I was temporarily granted permission to stay in the family home with the children. The house was however in his name so I knew my time at that residence would be limited. I moved quickly to find an apartment and then to seek out help with the move.

While the stuff was slowly disappearing right under my nose, I was actually able to lock down a job at the hospital and my mother helped me with the first and last month's security deposit. As these positive turn of events of becoming independent were occurring, the childish war between my abuser and the neighbor commenced which unfortunately left me dangling in the middle.

Now I had child protective in my life and the processes of family court. My lawyer maintained a great amount of confidence while child protective assured me that I was doing the right thing. The routine of checking the new apartment had gone well however in court they tried to settle by awarding joint custody - something I knew would never work as he wouldn't be capable of acting civil or even keeping his distance.

With disregard of my well-being, the neighbor would engage my abuser by threats of burning down his house and vice versa. Looking back; it really was the battle of the narcissists. Here were two completely similar men playing phone tag and road rage as I was truly lost somehow in the mix while trying to keep my feet on the ground and moving forward.

My desperation to make it on my own and stay out of the abuser's home was very prominent. I knew these petty wars were running its course between the two men but I wanted nothing to do with it. The neighbor and his wife would actually make suggestions that we ought to convince my abuser that we were having threesomes because they believed it would be funny. Here I was thinking that what it would really do is cause an even bigger trigger and put me in the direct line of danger and I really wanted no involvement with the chaos they were steadily creating. What I really wanted was calmness, quiet, the ability to begin healing and to be left alone so that I could succeed. By trusting that family to help me when my intuition suggested not to, I set myself up to fail.

On my original application for the hospital, I never reported an old charge that I assumed was thrown out. Because of my failure to report an old misdemeanor, they had to suspend me until I was able to provide further paperwork to clear myself. Only 2 weeks out of the home and into my own apartment, I was now faced with the numbing reality that I had no income to provide for myself or my children. I was lucky enough to have food stamp assistance but I knew this wouldn't pay the bills. The confusion from the neighbor and the abuser had taken its toll on me as well. They had so much of their own agendas running such a course that I could barely comprehend what the hell was going on anymore. Their back and forth actually seemed more personal to them and the goal as it appeared was to prove who is the bigger moron. Everything from shooting bags of flour across the store to frantic midnight phone calls of threats had occurred between the two men.

There was no doubt that I had to step away from either side. The craziness was over-the-top and rather uncalled for. While they played out their little game, I was left to the reality of having to throw in the towel and return back to the abuser's home because I couldn't expect my mother to pay the month-to-month rent and the other bills as well. The job search for other employment wasn't producing any results and the clearance process from the hospital job wasn't processing fast enough.

The night I made that choice to return to the abuser's house was the hardest decision I had to make. I couldn't at that moment foresee any other way. However disheartening; I was certain that I had at least tried and that my mistakes were from sloppy decision making on my behalf. The desperation to break free clouded my better judgment, if I had taken more careful steps, I probably would of been more successful.

I saw myself again at the age of 5 standing at that tree while the tempestuous storm shot lightening down all around me. The rain impaled me like bullets and yet I stood there numb to the impact. The words *so close* flashed before me and I just hung my head in defeat. I began to wonder if I would ever become truly free - as free as the rabbit and butterflies who continued forward into those tranquil fields of peace, warmth and calmness. As the darkness clouded me yet again, that one monarch still fluttered nearby and I looked towards her and told myself that someday I will be that monarch; scarred from the struggle yet beautiful, and free.

Chapter 7

*"Many of life's failures are people who did not
realize how close they were to success when they gave up."*

~ Thomas Edison

In order to become successful with a major change in your life, you must first accept that it won't come easy. In total, I had 9 failed attempts of leaving and you better believe that every failure wasn't received very well. The set backs are discouraging and heartbreaking because you continue to convince yourself that you will never break out of his prison. Some attempts were well planned, and some were impulsive acts of desperation and some were completely flawed from the start but instead of looking at the amount of attempts in a negative manner, I chose to recognize that I wasn't willing to give up.

The aftermath of losing the hospital job and the apartment set me into a very gray outlook. I had however gotten out far enough to make it through court hearings and obtain a job. Now the abuser actually went out of his way to overdo the honeymooning phase. The lies of loving me and being sorry for all of the abuse and nonsense came at me from many directions but there I sat unconvinced and knowing how tall those lies were. The only good thing that came as a result of that situation was conceiving my youngest daughter. By conceiving her, I was given even more of a reason to finally escape hell in one piece.

Now I had the opportunity to sit back and assess my previous mistakes.

The biggest mistake was desperation and going against my own instincts. I now knew that no running into the night nor depending on shallow promises was the key. With or without outside support, I had to really focus on what to do and where I will go. The first and most obvious would be to get a job and then to find a temporary place to stay until I could go on my own. By using diversions, I was able to get his focus elsewhere while I built back the confidence to make it through those very important steps. I kept his focus with the online nonsense because I knew he would be so jealous that he wouldn't be able to see past his ignorant assumptions. It's both funny and sad how easy it actually was to use his own stupidity against him.

The problem I faced with the diversion was that he took it out on both myself and our kids. When he would fill up with that rage, sometimes he would flip out on our oldest son for the smallest things such as his eating food later at night. These outbursts would turn into actual fist fights in which I had to get between the both of them and suffer a few flying fists to the ribs or the head. The verbal assaults were just as nasty as he would call our older daughter such terms as 'slut' 'cunt' and 'whore'; the same names he'd often call me.

As if the verbal and physical violence wasn't enough, he often seemed to have a problem with the teenage kids leaving the house to have a social life. They too were being heavily isolated.

There were moments where I had to cover up for either my daughter or oldest son so that they could get out. When it was later discovered, my ass was handed to me while objects were violently thrown across the room. He was also against allowing them to learn how to drive. Any mention or request seemed to really set him off in giant fits of rage. If they mentioned that they wanted to look for a job, again the anger flew because any change of income meant a change in his food stamp benefits. It was like he wanted to disable every one of us from ever having a life. My second oldest son had reached a point of intolerance for the abuse within the house and would leave school and stay with his cousin in town. Though I did worry about him, I really couldn't blame him. Who would want to come to a home filled with chaos, violence, name-calling and dysfunction?

Now carefully trying to plan my way out; watching what the kids were turning into gave me even more reason. As a result from not getting out sooner, they were susceptible to a very unstable and abusive environment. They now think it's perfectly normal to lie and have become a product of their surroundings. These types of children can easily grow into a 'Cluster-B personality disorder.' Where I thought I was helping them by the self sacrifices, I was really causing them harm.

On one of the numerous times in the past, one night I had to call the police because he and his twin brother were attacking me. The fight originated virtually out of nowhere and was yet another one of those violent altercations where I can't even tell you what triggered it. As I managed to dial 9-1-1, he continually punched me in the head and ripped the phone out of the wall. I knew the call did get through so I managed to somehow escape him and his brother and run down the driveway to wait for the responding police. He followed me and continued to attempt another go at me until moments later, the officer shows up. I go through the process of explaining the altercation while he yelled and rambled that it was all my fault. The officer thankfully knew better and sent him to his partner who showed up a moment later. The officer then told me that he knew my abuser and knows he is violent and asked me if I wished to press charges. While my children were there crying, I denied pressing charges and the cop looked at me sternly and said "If I have to come out here again, we are removing your children because you are unwilling to arrest the problem, are you sure you don't want to press charges?"

Now I want you to sit back and think about what that officer was telling me. I also want you to think about how I mentioned above that my older kids have become the product of their environment. I also want you to think about the beginning of my story where I mentioned that my mother was abused and I witnessed it. Are you starting to see the cycle?

I did grow up in an abusive home, and I did think at one time it was normal. My kids grew up in an abusive home and they too think that it is normal. Is it really a wise choice to stay in the abusive relationship for the kids? Are you *really* helping them by staying?

It hurts me to admit it because I was so beaten down and used and isolated but by not leaving back when my baby was beaten out of me, I became a partly catatonic prisoner by staying around a man who continually abused me. My kids grew up witnessing it, and they were attacked themselves. It's a bitter, yet brutal fact that you have got to accept if you think staying for the kids is a good idea. I understand exactly where your mind is at, because mine was also there. The abusers work so hard at convincing you of such worthlessness that you can barely see beyond that sick and persistent mental programming. If you have children and you cannot muster the confidence to care about yourself, then please do it for your children or else they too may become his victims.

Let me open your eyes up some more now. A child will want acceptance from his or her abusive father. When you begin to make those steps out that door, he will use their need for acceptance against you by pretending to change for them. He will coerce them and lie to them and they are unbelievably naive and easy targets. He manipulated you didn't he so how hard would it be for him to do that to his own kids? Despite your years of sacrifice and defending them, they will actually turn against you! All it takes are promises, a bit of freedom, failing to give them any rules or guidelines, allowing them to do whatever they want with whoever they want and buying them whatever they want. You may have to face the very painful fact that you probably have to leave without them.

Do not think he won't use them as a way to try and lure you back because he will. Just like he saw you, they are objects to him and not people.

In a situation like this, you really have to walk away. There is nothing more you can do for those kids because like you, they will have to learn on their own.

I cannot pretend that any of this came easy for me. I've had sleepless nights where a very small part of my mind would make me feel guilty because of those kids. The truth however was that if I had stayed for them then I was willing to give up my own life - I had spent far too long putting myself last for the children who were no longer capable of recognizing how much sacrifice was given. He worked too hard for too long at manipulating them for his own selfish needs and from there, I reached a plateau of brutal reality by acknowledging that there was nothing else I could possibly do.

There will come a point in your situation where you will know you are ready. You may be exactly like me and have done so many things wrong. You may have even tried to leave in the past but he either talked you back or you had no other choice within your reach but you will finally make it to a point where nothing will stop you. The kids will no longer be the excuse nor will not knowing where to go. It is eerily similar to when you know you are ready to quit smoking and do it cold turkey. Come hell or high water, you are ready for the change and will do whatever it takes to succeed.

When I got to that point; it was brutal recognition of the bigger picture in a whole. Not only were the children suffering, but I was so withdrawn from life that my outlook was a very dull and hopeless one. I could barely see that single monarch in the distance fluttering around but she was still in sight. She was there to remind me that just over this last mountain was a colorful valley filled with the same tranquility and shelter that the rabbit discovered. It was a valley of hope and a promise of fulfilling dreams if I could only stand up on my own two feet and begin my journey towards it.

Obstacles are however overwhelming and with a lack of resources, I knew that I had better seek the tools it would take to conquer that towering mountain.

One wintry night during the Christmas season, it occurred to me that a church was a great place to start obtaining real life interaction skills. This request would be innocent enough and harmless enough to my abuser that he would be blind to what my real goal was.

By January, he took my request serious enough to attend the Sunday services at a neighboring Presbyterian church. After four Sundays, the idea of attending couldn't no longer be a real option as he found a way to engage in a dispute with one of its members. Though I wouldn't call myself an overboard Christian, I recognized that the person to person interaction was very healthy despite the subject. It was another avenue where I discovered that nobody else had viewed me as negatively as he did and this was yet another empowering moment of surviving his abuse.

No matter your religious beliefs, there exists a sensation of enlightenment while surrounded by those who seek out the good in life. The strength in their faith is inspiring and it inspires you to delve inside of yourself to see that despite everything you were conditioned to believe, that there exists a light within you. All of us have probably learned that all children were born as innocents and we hear these stories that perhaps the work of the devil turns an innocent into anything but. With being reintroduced to these very basic teachings of the bible, this also taught me to forgive and let go.

I had spent too many years under his thumb and bitter with the situation. I had nothing but anger, hate, and questions such as "why me?" but by dwelling on what he was doing, it disabled me from making any progress.

Later that summer he discovered a church where we could actively visit without his shortcomings spoiling it. Within that group of people, I strengthened my knowledge on learning how to not only to forgive but to as well move on without the abuser in a healthy way. In many of their programs, they offered weekly groups for various types of situations and I was able to sit in with a group focused on emotionally healthy women.

While listening to the struggles of these other women and their terrific tales of surviving through it by using their passionate belief of Jesus, something occurred to me. I had the belief within myself already, but I was denying myself my own full potential. Somehow, I needed to create my own Jesus and by that I mean this: I had to find my one driving force, my object of passion that would take my hand and walk through hell with me and wash away those fears and self-doubt. Like the women that I was surrounded by in group, I began to pray for clarity and strength and once I began to fill with the optimism,

I continued to pray for a job. I applied for the openings at a school, a casino, and a factory. There wasn't much he could do to prevent my attempts, we were so poor that I was begging my mother to help me with some bills so that the kids were taken care of. I felt like a beggar but I continued to pray nevertheless trying to ride the waves of a total positive outlook; my Jesus would hear me and somehow he will see that 21 years was too long to be confined.

Three nail-biting months of total poverty came and went when one afternoon, I received a call from the local casino and the woman explained that I was chosen to work in their new location in Chittenango. There aside me appeared that singular monarch as my heart fluttered - all of those long sleepless nights of frantic worry were coming to an end.

Again, I pictured my 5 year old self back at that tree with the rabbit, the butterflies and dragonflies. The tempestuous storm was now passing and the field was now regaining warmth and color. The one monarch descended and landed on my shoulder. The rabbit hopped over to me and the rest of the butterflies and dragonflies cheerfully flew around. The freedom to proceed into the tranquil field had now come forth. Whether it was answered prayers, or perseverance, there is one thing I do know with certainty.

I had too many chances to give up, and give in. I had the opportunity to remain quietly in a home filled of abuse and let myself die but I knew by doing so, that I would have given up on myself. I saw hope from watching my parents find real love, by seeing friends have healthy relationships and by simply knowing deep down that life doesn't have to feel like a prison sentence. I knew that I was capable of love and that I was worth it and it would ultimately take my ability to forgive, let go, and step forward into a new life to obtain it.

Once you can forgive, and fully let go of the past and all of the ugliness within it, you are no longer chained down. Just continue to repeat those words: *Never give up.*

Chapter 8

"Real freedom is creative, proactive, and will take me into new territories. I am not free if my freedom is predicated on reacting to my past."

~ Kenny Loggins

My job at the new casino started out with a bang. With all of the excitement, and the noise of the slot machines, their tag-line was a simple, but daily positive reminder; "Where all of your hopes and dreams just might come true!"

I made immediate friendships although our shift was the day-killer with hours from 4 in the afternoon until 12:30 in the morning. I could sense magic in the air, and often found myself smiling and really enjoying myself without worrying of being questioned as to why I was so happy. If ever I smiled around my abuser, he would tear it apart until there was nothing left of the moment. To really feel the excitement of being happy, truly happy, it felt like heaven. It was as simple as a complement from a guest or even my supervisors complementing me on a job well done. Because of these very simple key factors, I threw my passion into my work and discovered a plethora of strengths I had long ago lost.

The end of each night was met a certain level of sadness as I now knew that I would have to return to a prison until 3:30 the next afternoon. The drive home really felt like chains being reassigned to their positions - I'd wonder what sort of complaint I would be faced with when walking through that door. Usually, I was met with the questioning as to why it had taken me so long to get back home. He insisted that he knew exactly how long it takes and that I should consider walking.

His threats of taking the vehicle away from me were quite frequent. At this final stage however; as he spoke, it sounded like distant mutters going in one ear and out of the other. I was just unwilling to accept anything he had to speak over me. I hadn't even loved him for 19 or those 21 years and he really just lost full control of me because I was too empowered to be kicked down any further. When I questioned my own strength, or wondered if this choice wouldn't be the best for the children, I would remember the lowest points in that relationship.

By thinking about all of the things he had done to me, I saw with clarity that his pattern had never changed, but had only sometimes slowed down. It was mostly accusations, abuse, mental programming, and other means of manipulation but never once was it actual love of any kind.

During my last and final camping trip with him; it was too obvious to myself that I had truly let go and moved on.

While one of my favorite activities is camping, I couldn't for a moment find excitement during the entire trip. The moments I had with my kids made it doable. I could at least experience their moments of happiness while making s'mores or enjoying the nearby beach. It was however short lived because even the use of provided food angered him. If one of the kids wanted more than one s'more, it was a tragedy to him and it would escalate to unnecessary levels. However much he thought he was gaining by acting like a continual asshole, his attempts were null and void to me. My sympathy showed for my children. In no way did they deserve the belittlement for being a kid and desiring more than one treat around the campfire. He was receiving food-stamps for the family, so I could never understand why it was such a dreadful tragedy for the children to enjoy the food those benefits provided.

Towards the end of that specific camping trip, a horrendous storm impaled the campsite while I was at work. It rolled off of Oneida Lake and dumped its energy directly on that area - although I worried for my children who were unsurprisingly forced to care for the site after the storm by themselves, I took the irony of the tempestuous storm as the last page of his tyranny. To me, it signified that it had passed over my head and was now behind me. Those dark clouds had now diminished and revealed the sun in all of its glory. My path was coming to light and there was nothing that could stop my momentum.

Another revelation came through the assistance of the church. Because of my certainty, I opted to be counseled by one of the senior pastors as an attempt to work at recovery. The vision of freedom adorned my mind in hopeful pools of positive thoughts.

She sat down with me in the beginning with the assumption that perhaps I wanted to try to heal my relationship with the abuser. No more than 10 minutes into the session, she understood that the relationship couldn't be saved. While in conversation, I confessed that I was completely aware that people have no idea how he really is and that's when she stopped me. She assured me that despite the guise he thought he wore, people were aware that he wasn't the person he was trying to portray. My suspicions were correct, people were able to see beyond his many masks and hopefully were smart enough to see through his lies and manipulations. After all, not everyone is that lost 16 year old homeless kid who doesn't know any better.

In a composition book that I would leave in my locker at work, I began devising a plan to get out on my own. I would also bring a tablet with me so that I could research how much the average amount was for rent while estimating the cost of utilities, food, gas and other practical needs.

My salary didn't appear to be large enough to carry me and that caused me some worry though I wouldn't lose sight of what I was working towards. If anything, I knew I could resort to receiving additional assistance from the county and work towards a better position in the company where I could earn more money.

The problem with gaining strength is the abuser's ability to notice that he no longer has a hold on you. While I diligently worked towards my goal, he came to realize that nothing he said or did would phase me. This heightened the tension at home while I was away. The fighting between him and our teenage daughter was rising out of control. He would leave not long after I left to work which left her responsible for my then 4 year old daughter and also the preparation of food and other needs. He would constantly be absent from home; this stripped away any chance my teenage daughter had at a social life.

She had an obvious right to feel a level of anger towards him but because teenagers can often react out of impulse, the arguments soon grew into a ticking time bomb. This situation left me in a tricky position. I knew damn well that he was pushing the older kids in a selfish attempt to cause me to leave my job. As my daughter complained, I tried to explain to her that it was best to back off and let him rage because he'd eventually stop. The truth was that I really had no way of knowing how bad the fights were in the home while I was gone, but I was aware that they were occurring. Something told me that they would escalate to the heights that they would reach when he fought with me.

My oldest son would tell me that my daughter would start most of the fights because of her need to speak with her boyfriend. My daughter would deny triggering him but somehow I believed that she was indeed pushing his buttons. Whatever the case, this collaboration was like pouring gasoline on top of an uncontrolled wild fire.

His outbursts of anger towards me grew to a constant existence. It took all I was worth not to react because I knew he'd already gone rounds with the teenage kids. As I'd get ready for work, the belittling and continued accusations flew out of him in a consistency that polluted the entire house. The kids were yelling and screaming, he was yelling and flipping out, and even my youngest daughter was throwing stuff around and thinking this was normal. The toxic aroma was trying to cloud me as it was too constant which made it impossible to ignore.

One afternoon as I arrived to work, my expression surely showed it as my supervisor took me to the side. In a flit of tears, I broke down and explained to her the hell I was enduring and she talked with me about how she had lived through the exact same situation.

She offered me advice that was rather brilliant though I never got the time to do it myself. She explained how she moved objects out of her house slowly such as the children's birth certificates and other important paperwork like titles for motor vehicles that were rightfully hers. She also mentioned how she put back any money that she could once a week (even if it was 5 dollars or so) and how it would add up over time. She also mentioned that she knew somebody who found a car at a reasonable price and offered to direct me to him if I should need that sort of assistance. She then handed me a pamphlet from our employer which offered counseling and services for battered and abused women. As I wiped my tears, and then listened to her story of survival, it occurred to me that I was never once alone. There are so many of us out there who are left to face this battle in the deception of love. We are fooled and used after our hearts were broken. They promise us love, happiness, and total commitment and then change when they're comfortable. This realization didn't set me back, rather, it empowered me even more.

I learned that she got out even though she didn't have a lot of money. She was able to get on her own two feet and start over much like my own mother did back when she divorced my father. Here were these two examples of success staring me in the face telling me that I too can get there.

With the advice that the supervisor gave me, I formulated that into my composition book and jotted down items that I could sneak into my work locker without looking like I was moving into the place. This brilliant idea had however come to me a little too late as the friction at home between my daughter and my abuser spun way out of control.

On October 21st 2015, I prepared for work like any other day while the abuser screamed at my daughter for using a video game system as opposed to cleaning her room. This chaos was aggravating though not much different from any other day of their petty arguments and I proceeded to work after explaining to her that she should just let it go. I gave my youngest daughter a hug and kiss like I usually did before getting into the van and leaving. I had no idea that this was the day that I would conquer a 21 year old mountain.

Following my usual procedure, I took my backpack and jacket to my locker and checked in with my co-workers to prepare for my shift. That Wednesday at work began like any with a litter of the usual guests on the gaming floor and typical staffing to expect in the middle of the week. In my normal routine, I began my rounds by checking the restrooms to see what was needed when I immediately noticed that my smart phone was vibrating repeatedly in my pant pocket. At this point I was officially on the clock so I initially ignored it until reaching the second restroom area. Once I checked a few stalls, I decided I had better see who was trying so hard to get my attention.

After unlocking the phone, my biggest fear was staring at me in the face. My oldest son was in a manic frenzy trying to alert me that the abuser had violently attacked my teenage daughter, and even the family pet.

I was now in an immediate panic as I quickly ran off of the game floor to the closest employee exit behind the building. Without hesitation, I called the house to discover that it really had happened though my son was hesitant to dial 911. His refusal caused me to dial emergency and explain everything as best as I could while trying to remain as calm as possible. Everything began unfolding before me as the years and years of struggling with the abuse myself had now fully washed over onto my daughter as well. Whether she triggered him or not, he had gone overboard by hitting her in front of my 4 year old daughter, 11 year old and 19 year old son.

After hanging up with the emergency dispatcher, I felt the flood of fear rush over me as I shook uncontrollably. Several of my co-workers came out to see if I was okay but I sat in a metal chair to the side of the wall and allowed myself to lose it. I needed to feel the pain from the reality of what was occurring in that very toxic atmosphere. One of my female co-workers told me that she was also once a victim of similar circumstances and she commended me for facing my fear and taking the steps to report the violent altercation.

My next thought was the realization that there was no going back. While fighting through the heightened terror from my PTSD, I had one of my co-workers help me out until I was calm enough to make it to my vehicle. In that short and terrifying walk to my van, the casino's tag-line screamed in my head "where all of your hopes and dreams just might come true!"

In an old yet routine habit, I drove from the casino to a nearby park to sort myself out and think. I knew that my two younger children were still in his house and I needed a place to go. Unsure of what my next steps would be, I called a friend who I'd been real close to from work who happened to have the day off that specific day. In my momentum of uncontrollable fear, I knew that by talking to him, I could reach a reasonable level of thought. He was somebody I really enjoyed my time with while at work. He could always make me laugh and make me think. He was also somebody who really believed in me and encouraged me. Hearing his voice was enlightening to say the least; I rambled out my fears and what had happened and explained how I felt unsure of what to do next. He listened and apologized for not being close enough to help. Though I truly needed him to be there to assist me, it was actually better that I was left to press forward on my own.

Another friend was aware of how bad things had become and so I reached out to her. I was lucky that she offered to let me stay at her home until I could get on my own feet. From there I gathered my teenage daughter and oldest son and met with my friend, and together we all went to the police station. I couldn't stand the thought of my two younger kids still in his house, the teens and I explained the living conditions within the house and the officer had thankfully assisted me with removing the two younger kids. I walked into that house with the officer wearing my work outfit and I asked her if I could at least grab some clothing for the children and myself. She thankfully gave me enough time to grab a laundry basket and I filled it with clothing for 4 children and myself and that wasn't much. I also grabbed a small box full of my illustration pencils and a sketchpad and that would be the only items I had left that home with. Other work outfits, a box filled with charcoal pencils, and a sketchpad.

In the days that followed; I petitioned the court for full custody of my two younger children and filed for a stay-away order of protection. They awarded my teenage daughter with a full stay-away but kept mine to a refrain-from order which meant that if he saw me, he could still come near me.

In our first court date to follow soon after, the judge recommended that we worked it out in a civil matter though I knew there wasn't any civility with working with this man. He refused to allow me to have anything else of mine such as clothing and photographs of sentimental value and of course tried to say he was sorry and that he didn't hit our daughter.

The whole bullshit line soon followed thereafter with promises of changing and of course blaming the kids for the issues but never once could he admit to what he had done. If he couldn't blame me, he'd blame the kids and yet refused to acknowledge that he was at fault. That had always remained a constant in those 21 years; the blame was shifted on to everybody but him. He also used people from the church during his attempts to drag me back. They would contact me without full knowledge of what had really happened and of course I tried to explain but the effort really wasn't worth it. No matter what he was throwing at me, I knew I was never going back. It no longer mattered to me what he was convincing other people of, because the truth is that they had no real idea of what it was like to live with a man who couldn't comprehend how to treat a woman or his own children. They hadn't once walked a day in my life to even have the ability to opinionate on me or the situation. All they had was a manipulated head full of his lies and what good would it do to waste any further energy on people he personally gaslighted and turned into flying monkeys, shame shifters, smear campaigners and bullies.

You'll be amazed at how free you feel when you come to realize that none of it has any power over you any longer. All those years of feeling chained down will begin to fade away and fall behind you as you progress into the new phase of your life.

For 21 years, a man tried to make me feel like an insignificant and meaningless existence and he tried to own me like an object but I didn't let him succeed. For 19 of those years, I had no love for him and I thought I was doing what was best for my children. For 15 of those years, I moved on mentally and worked at healing myself because I knew deep down that I was better than the situation. Most of those years I thought I was doing it alone. For some of those years I thought death was my only way out. For this year, I know I am a survivor and that I will never let somebody have that sort of control over me ever again.

Chapter 9

"Each day is a new day, a new opportunity to
work towards making your life the way you want it."

~ Josie Cluney

I used to have reveries of what real love would be like if I were ever to become so lucky. During my earlier days of writing; I would formulate the vision of a man within my mind who was normally faceless and I would give him the characteristics of what I believed to be true love.

In these stories, he was typically rather funny, and often calm during any stressful situations. There was never any sort of confrontation nor yelling. It was indeed a fantasy similar to something you may read in a romance novel where he would spontaneously bring home a collection of roses and chocolates. I'd daydream that he adored the classical works of Bach or Chopin much like myself or enjoy a rainy afternoon while I rested in his arms and recited my own poetry to him. He'd also fancy long peaceful walks through the forest hand in hand as he told me about his thoughts and dreams. Sometimes he'd fix a candlelit dinner and make a path of rose petals to the warm waiting bath accompanied with some fine picked chardonnay and of course strawberries we could both enjoy. Most importantly, he'd make me the center of his universe and cherish everything about me without ever hurting me in any fashion.

What was once but a reverie began unfolding before my eyes. While growing closer to one of my co-workers, I came to realize that I was falling in love. Afraid that I would be stepping out of one hell, and into another, I literally feared the realization that I was falling fast and hard. My ability to trust anyone was long since gone in the abyss and yet, I somehow found it easy to trust this man who was otherwise soft-spoken and tender-hearted.

He had no way of knowing what lie ahead as he was aware that I was trapped for 21 years with the abuser. The fear of what was to come was great, but we were immediately quite open and honest with another. What I discovered was that he too was hurt on many occasions in the past, some of which were similar pains to my own and in a sense, this level of understanding brought us closer.

Though we both recognized that we were falling deeply in love, we both chose to take our time. There was no need to rush something this wonderful yet all I really wanted to do was to let go and run into his arms.

We'd spend hours talking about everything from the paranormal to music and our lives before we met. It felt wonderful to have this man who actually listened to me without shutting me up. I had never before experienced a relationship where it was obvious that I was extremely important to the person I am with. He actually cared about my likes, my desires, my thoughts and dreams. The reality that this was actually happening and not just some reverie jotted down in one of my short stories was so overwhelming that I didn't really know how to perceive it.

I had immediate fears that somehow in some way I would screw up much like how my abuser had always told me that I couldn't be loved. I'd search my mind for ways to fix whatever was broken about me but once I had explained that to him, he made me see that there's nothing wrong with me what so ever. There was a night that I cried myself to sleep because I was so afraid that somehow I would screw it up.

He helped me to see that I could talk with him about anything that was on my mind, and that is exactly how I began to deeply trust him.

While I would like to tell you that there's some magical wand that mends you once you have left the abuser, that really isn't the case. From living through so much abuse, some of that ugliness would cloud me as my new relationship progressed. One major struggle I faced was attempting to handle my doubt. I was still living with my friend who wanted me to check out other avenues such as online dating and meeting specific men with great careers. What she couldn't understand was that I had fallen in love with someone from work who actually understood the sensitivity of my situation.

Some people who want to help you will sometimes formulate their ideas into what they think is best for you but those people don't take the time to include you in those plans. As this was happening, I felt like I was being told what to do which was nothing that I wanted for myself. In hindsight; I felt like I had walked out of prison and into a concentration camp where I wasn't given the time to think and act for myself. Fortunately I had the tools to understand what she was trying to do and pulled myself away from that. The reminder of the neighbors and their own ideas was constantly at the forefront of my mind and so I understood that staying in the friend's home would be as temporary as possible. I was out! No way was I going to let anyone cast their chains into my life ever again; not even a so-called friend who would rather tell me instead of asking me.

My resources were tightly limited. My abuser had taken the vehicle that my mother had helped me to get and the friend was temporarily lending me her personal vehicle; a Jeep which had several problems with it. The most concerning issue were the tires which looked like they belonged on a very small car. Just envision in your head a Jeep with 16 inch rims fitted with tires from one of those tiny Fiats. In a kind act for my own safety; my co-worker actually purchased a brand new set of tires so that I could safely get around without fearing that one of those really small tires would blow out. One would think that this very generous purchase would at least be seen for what it really was - an act of kindness and nothing more.

114

In a flit of irrational thinking, the friend had told other people that the tires were purchased with the assumption that she'd have to return the favor in sexual acts. It seems a little sick to me as I think about this moment. My abuser had often rambled off sick sexual fantasies or accusations about people that I had only glanced at innocently. These delusions of his would always spark up a fight or further accusations which made no actual sense. Now my own friend was acting in the same fashion and for no logical reason. Perhaps it is safe to say that this says a lot about them as people and how they view the world. What I can say to you reading this is that you are under no obligation to inherit someone else's problems. When you have come to the point where you faced your fear and left the abuse, it will shock you how many other people you begin to remove from your life. Going no-contact is more productive than being attached to negative sources.

These little things about the friend concerned me to the point where I discussed with my co-worker that the situation wasn't working in her house. To spare me from facing a bigger problem in this new situation; he willingly began aiding me in a search for a new home so that I would have total control over myself and surroundings.

From driving around to leaving inquiries with local realtors; I diligently searched everything from single-wide trailers to apartment listings using the resources available from the Community Action program. The county welfare services office also provided me with a list of landlords and their phone numbers. The discovery process in the search wasn't exactly immediate; most places were either unavailable, or they had a significant wait. I wouldn't however let this set me back as I knew I had the choice and it was mine alone.

After about a week and a half, I began to receive offers to view the potential locations of my future home. What I was being presented with were fixer-uppers owned by a man I would describe as the area's rumor mill. As I desperately flirted with the thought of having this attempt at remodeling a very ran down house; the co-worker told me to take my time and really think about what I would be getting into.

Even though you are moving forward by yourself, sometimes it is extremely important to reach out for help. You will recognize a person who is genuine versus someone who is careless of you. Also remember that making any choice is ultimately up to you. I took what he was saying to me into consideration because I already believed that those specific houses would have been a bad choice. There was too much needed work on top of the landlord who had no problem telling me about the shortcomings of previous tenants.

When you come across someone who is trying to offer you something while cutting down the previous occupants, trust your instinct that they probably will do the same thing to you. When you are taking a step forward, always proceed with caution so that you don't wind up taking two steps back. Remember; you got this far and you can and will keep going if you take the time to think about your next steps.

During the search for my new home, the co-worker and I had grown so attached that we began a relationship together. We were both already very much in love with the other and had taken the time to learn each other. The differences of his mannerisms compared to my abuser was so great that I would suggest it was like comparing black to white.

In the first month with my abuser, I had felt alone and much like the effort of making things work was left up to me. He wasted no time coercing me into his bed and that experience was all about him. He didn't cuddle with me, or at least get to know much about me. All he wanted was for me to lie down on my back - this undoubtedly soon turned into a chore I'd never look forward to. The abuser also would let out his true side when it became difficult to hide his true self by calling me names or getting upset too quickly over nothing. The only conversations were made up of arguing or some memory of his about either how much better a former lover was or the stupidity of crimes that he and his brothers committed. With so much as a mention about noticing the one sidedness, the abuser would be quick to change the subject and could care less about my feelings. It was always all about him, period.

My co-worker is a completely different experience altogether. We had first become acquainted while working the same hours and typically having breaks around the same time. From this obvious connection we had grown together into a close friendship. He actually cared about how I felt and what was on my mind, and at first this intimidated me. I'd wonder if he only spoke to me because he wanted to have meaningless sex with me. I had grown so accustomed to being used for sex by the abuser that I partially expected that all men were the same way. As each day passed, I learned that this assumption wasn't the case with the co-worker. From worrying about if I had lunch for the shift to anything that may be weighing me down, he showed that he really cared by constantly asking. I wasn't asking this from him, nor was I really searching to become close to anybody. The attraction happened without any effort nor intent. The most beautiful aspect of this connection was how natural it was.

He worked aside me as I continued the search for a new home and since we had grown into a relationship, together we decided on a newly remodeled apartment.

However beautiful life had become, that small little existence of doubt still tried to raise its ugly head. These thoughts would race in the back of my mind because this new step in allowing myself to trust fully was a very scary step. I was certain of two facts without question. #1: I was never going back to the abuser or his home no matter what happens, and #2: I was deeply in love with the co-worker and already felt quite attached to him.

Engaging in a serious commitment after being held down so long in my past was an extreme challenge. I inherited a new freedom with a man who wouldn't dictate my every move - at first I really didn't know how to act.

The adjustment alone was quite a challenge; now I didn't have to walk on egg-shells or worry if I was a bit too long at the grocery store. The co-worker actually encouraged me to do things but the problem was that I didn't really know what to do with myself. I had spent so long confined with the abuser that I didn't actually have friends I could visit though luckily I made one good friend through my work at the paranormal society.

When first meeting her, I was petrified that I wouldn't know what to do or how to act. I was now very much in control of myself but because of the seclusion, breaking out of those former chains didn't come easy. Of course the initial meeting had went well as we met for lunch but I had also learned something from her that I wasn't previously aware of. Our work in the paranormal society was done online through a social media group. I had varying duties from website maintenance to writing educational articles on paranormal subjects. It was also expected of us to watch the conversations in the group's page as a way to keep the peace. By being an active representative, this meant that I was working with some 80 other reps on top of the 55,000+ members who came to the page. Even as a team member; I often kept to myself and maintained my focus on what was expected of me. Because I was in such a bubble, my friend explained to me that the other reps thought I was either snobby or unfriendly though neither was the case.

I learned that she also wondered what was going on with me. Before I left my abusive situation, she would invite me out to either lunch or dinner and I'd often decline. By her explaining these things to me; I came to see just how tucked away from the world he really had me. Later that evening, I cried in a deep mourning for the 21 years I had lost in my own life. There was so much that I had missed from the age of 16 to the age of 37 - the reality of that is something that I have to live with but also something that has taught me a real valuable lesson. Under no circumstances was I ever going to let another person take my freedom away from me again.

After that night; I decided to let go of those ugly feelings and continued to progress in my new life. I now have a wonderful man at my side and have repaired my relationships with family members who

I had long since missed. New friendships are also coming into fruition complete with people who share my same interests.

Even today there is that tiny sense of doubt hanging over me. My brain wants to think things like "this is all too good to be true" but then the co-worker often talks with me about those ugly feelings and we throw them away together. After all, no change comes immediate but from enough support, it comes one day at a time.

Chapter 10

"Don't dwell on what went wrong. Instead, focus on what to do next. Spend your energies on moving forward toward finding the answer."

~ Dennis Waitley

While moving forward I have noticed that my brain is still stuck in defensive mode. My first and biggest challenge was coming to terms with leaving the danger of the past behind me. I wanted to believe that once I began forward that everything will kind of fix itself, but that wasn't the case. I was lucky to have the co-worker for main support but I still needed a counselor. My fears were and are still intact and overwhelming.

Interaction with other people had become quite difficult. I no longer had to worry about the abuser attacking me but I had spent 21 years under lock and key. What I did to overcome this hurdle was simply continue trying. My past really wanted to tear me down with a vengeance. Those negative thoughts fumbled around my brain constantly and it was hard to surpass the feelings of giving in. Once my brain went through the stages of fear, I took steps forward one day at a time. If the co-worker wasn't there to listen to me, I wrote down what bad thought was stopping me and worked at getting past the hold it had on me.

One of the most helpful steps at productive interaction with other people was to overcome my fear with talking on the phone. Most of the 21 years I had become afraid of the abuser overhearing me on the phone because he would twist something innocent into something it wasn't. When I now speak on the phone, I am extremely hesitant and still look around myself until I realize that I am okay. My words come out slowly at first but I press through the anxiety until I am confident.

There are advocates through abuse recovery programs who can actually assist you with the troubles you are having. In my area; we have Community Action program, Victims of Violence, and Vera House. Do not be afraid to reach out to programs that are designed to help victims of domestic violence. As of so far, I have discovered that I have so many services made available to me such as free legal assistance. The social services building was where I had learned about the various programs - my suggestion is that you first start with social services because they will have the information you need. Most police agencies also have information designed to help victims of domestic violence. Once you get an order of protection in place; most courts will also direct you in the right path. Do not be afraid to ask for help; facing your recovery alone is a hell of a lot harder than you can imagine. The advocates are almost always survivors and will understand you and your needs. They can also set you up with counseling and some places can even get you shelter.

My next step was to cut off all contact without hesitation. The social media profiles went first. The one detail that I wasn't aware of was how easy it is for someone to geo-track you. If you have the messenger program for certain social media sites, delete it off of your cell phone immediately. They like to add your location if you're mobile without you even realizing it. Go into your cell phone and make sure to shut off the location, Bluetooth, and sharing capabilities. Most cell phone carriers can assist you with this if you can't figure out how to do it yourself. I myself had to go to my service provider's tech department for assistance. The abuser had used my mobile number to track me and he had also somehow gotten into my phone through the social media messenger service. With so much going on, I had never thought of the cell phone causing me any trouble; the second I got out I should have gotten a new number and permanently deleted any social media that the abuser was aware of.

It felt like encroachment, I had to give up my online presence to maintain my safety. He had my personal computer in his possession so he found ways to use the internet browser to retrieve passwords. For my important accounts, I changed the passwords and then built a new social media page to maintain contact with my family who lives out of town.

When I started the new online presence, I wasn't sure of who to trust and mostly added family. Within that pack of people; a cousin was actually feeding him information off of my new page and had even directed him to it.

It hurt to discover what the cousin was doing, but moving forward is a learning process. It taught me to be careful of who to trust from the past. I would like to tell you that people will understand the sensitivity of your situation as you are on your road to recovery but nothing is further from the truth. Be real careful when starting over; the abuser can turn mutual friends into his flying monkeys as a way to control you from a distance. My abuser understood there was (and still is) a stay-away order of protection so he couldn't get to me himself. In a ploy of a sick fashion, he used not only my own cousin but also my own son's social media profile. I was not surprised when I had figured it out; I was firm on the no contact and left him no other way to reach me.

He continues to try even now. If someone from my past tries to contact me, I shut it off before it even has a chance to begin. He employs enablers and flying monkeys to assist him in continuing to control me but is met with a brick wall. The most shocking of people in his little bucket of tricks was the church pastor and my own daughter. Be prepared to expect anything from anyone; do not let it get to you and do not give in.

Blame and shame shifting came next through past acquaintances. Their lack of knowing the truth of the situation is not my problem and I do not give them the energy. What I have come to learn is that most people do not have the slightest idea of what I had

really lived through and that is nothing I should be concerned about. Remember: everyone's opinion doesn't even matter because they aren't you and have no idea about the truth. Eventually they will realize that they were manipulated when the abuser's true colors come out and I will still be moving forward with positive people around me.

To remain positive, I have come to forgive the abuser. It's dreadful to view him as a person but that is all he is, a human being with some serious issues. By forgiving him, I am able to move on with my life without holding on to the past. There will never come a moment where I allow him back in my life. It is however soulfully cleansing to shed away the bitterness within myself. There's no way that I will forget what he has done to me and he will never have that power over me again. That chapter of my life is over and I press forward anew. Do not rush yourself to forgive, and do not let others tell you that you need to. We grieve and recover at our own speed and will do so when ready.

I am currently still in family court over the children; when I overhear them discussing his having rights, I feel repulsed. Co-parenting with the abuser will never be civil, and I am probably looking at years of his petty attempts to drag everything out but that's okay. He can use the legal system as another tool to manipulate but that is all he can do. He tries to demean my character by using the older children against me. This does bother me a great deal, but I also know that they don't know any better. There will come a day where they will realize what is really going on. For now, he will give them unlimited freedom and whatever they want to keep them at his every manipulated command. Anyone who can lower themselves to use children as a way to make themselves look good is going to one day face the creator. Fortunately, they cannot lie nor manipulate God and will get what they deserve on their judgment day.

As I mentioned in an earlier chapter, taking care of your personal health is extremely important. If your situation was anything like mine; you were probably convinced that seeing any type of doctor was a crime. I recall the abuser going out of his way to cut me down for actually making appointments not only for myself, but also the children. For some reason, he never wanted to accept that the children and I could catch a cold (or something worse.) If I had mentioned that I didn't feel so well, he'd lose his temper in 2 seconds and verbally shame and dissect me while insisting that I was making up the sickness.

Perhaps the real issue was that he was frightened that I would confess my abuse to the doctor. Certainly the other fear was that even if I hadn't spoken up, the doctor would have realized somehow what was going on.

There is actual validity to the thought of a medical professional developing any suspicion. If like myself you have been exposed to long-term isolation, verbal, emotional and mental abuse, there's a very real chance that you might be suffering from either complex-post traumatic stress disorder or PTSD. Some of the symptoms associated with C-PTSD/PTSD are very recognizable if the attending physician looks close enough. Some common symptoms are guilt, shame, self-blame, feelings of mistrust and betrayal, hopelessness, depression, suicidal feelings and thoughts, physical aches and pains. These are only some of the symptoms; please do not self diagnose yourself and always seek out professional help if you believe you may be suffering from C-PTSD/PTSD.

Do not let yourself go. Feel the fear and respect it but do not let it corner you into a place you can't escape. Keep on top of your health and remember to do it for yourself. Release those old feelings of entrapment and love yourself again.

It was just about 3 months after leaving before I even considered taking care of my own health. We often forget about ourselves until it's too late. I've actually suffered a stroke during the writing process of this book - I was shopping with my father, step-mother, and youngest daughter when a sudden onset of dizziness overcame me. Confusion came next while I slowly made it outside of the store.

The world spun, my heart pounded and I was beginning to lose the feeling in my left arm. My initial thought was that I had made it so far only to have the world ripped from me in an instant. Despite that alarming fear, I fought it with my all but as I underwent this terrifying medical emergency; one thing really stood out at the forefront of my mind.

Life isn't a guarantee and it really is short. We don't really know if tomorrow is promised to us as we take things for granted. While I lie in the hospital bed recovering; it dawned on me that a large portion of my life was taken away from me by a man. That period of my life, I will never get it back and I want people to learn from me. The time you lose simply cannot be recovered. There's no reversal, nor magical wand to replace the years lost. Do not become suspended into your own negative thoughts; reach out for help and find ways to make that very important call because he isn't going to change for you. In 21 years, my abuser pretended to change but he steadily got much worse. I understand where your thoughts are, and why you might hesitate and procrastinate but what if one day your tomorrow wasn't promised? Please take care of yourself, you are not alone, and you are loved by many.

Chapter 11

"You are very powerful, provided you
know how powerful you are."

~Yogi Bhajan

I learned about how to spot a liar and how to let them know that I know better. By observation; I learned the telltale signs of a defensive person who is trying to hide something. I understood the clear patterns of a cheater and know that I will never allow myself to live through that again. I learned to trust my inner instincts and to never go against them. I discovered patience and how to withstand an explosive situation without reacting poorly on emotion.

A liar will assume that he or she can fool you despite the ridiculousness of their story. They will also assume that you will not question them and will often change their story up later. They will tell you that you are the one who remembers it incorrectly and will continue to convince you until you practically believe them over your own mind. They will exhibit changes in their behavior and often may answer your questions in very short answers without adding too many details. Sometimes they say "no" a lot and look away from you. They may even close their eyes or say "no" typically after hesitating. They may sometimes speak faster, and louder as they have become stressed. If something seems amiss to you about their story, ask them to tell it backward. If there's any truth to what they are saying, retelling it backward wouldn't be hard for them. Most importantly; listen to them more than you speak. A liar will talk a lot more in the assumption that they can win you over. Once you realize that you have caught them in a lie, don't hesitate to believe that they are probably lying about a lot of things. Have the respect for yourself in knowing that you deserve better. Your partner should love you and would never dream of lying to you, because what good would that do? Once you lose trust, what do you really have?

Someone who loves you correctly would not hide anything from you. If you notice that they become defensive; they are most likely trying to prevent you from discovering the truth about something. This can sometimes be worse than lying because they are trying hard to cover up something that they believe you will never uncover. They don't want you to know because then you will come upon something that's most likely deceptive and even destructive. They could be hiding another lover or a bad habit such as drugs. You could chance it by confronting them but if he's already abused you;

inherit that knowledge and empower yourself by leaving. You have to reach a point where you know and believe that you deserve to be treated better than that. If you are in a relationship then there shouldn't be any fear in being open with another. If he's keeping secrets then that is driving a wedge between the both of you and that can become counterproductive. A person who truly loves you will include you in absolutely everything.

One of the more bitter moments in any abusive situation is catching him cheating. The easiest way to discover that truth is when he begins to accuse you. There is so much guilt within him from doing the act himself that he will belittle you and accuse you to get the attention off of him. An even worse discovery is when you realize he treats her better than he does you. Those ever so famous words will fly out of his mouth "so-and-so is better than you" and he will make you feel inferior. In love; there is no competition nor room for making your partner feel like they have to compete for you. It is my opinion that once they cheat, the relationship is lost. That very act blows any trust out of the water, and what's worse is how they will treat someone else better even if temporarily. You're being made to sit home with children and afraid of having any sort of life outside of that house while he is free to do whatever he wants. Can't you see how demeaning that really is to you?

I also want you to think about this: If you are a teenage girl and a man much older than you is persistent on getting with you, take a step back and really think about it. I understand that he may offer you money, cigarettes, car rides or perhaps you are even angry with your parents and want revenge ... I get it. I *was* you. A much older man whom I called throughout this story *the abuser* pursued me with all of those promises and money and alcohol and look where it landed me. Because I thought these things were important, I spent 21 years being controlled, manipulated, dehumanized, isolated, chained down, secluded, belittled, and used. If you think you have it bad with your parents, just imagine what it is like being me. Do you really think it's worth it?

Under no circumstances should a much older man want a thing to do sexually with an underage girl. They have a name for the ones who do; they are called pedophiles. They prey on teens and children for their own selfish needs and have no consideration for the well-being nor feelings of their victims. Do not make the same foolish mistakes that I had in my most vulnerable moments; if you are having problems with a man seeking you out then tell somebody about it. There are people out there who can help you; if you can't tell your parents then tell someone at school or even the police. Know that you are worth much more than to be someone's toy or sex object.

It is not okay for us to set ourselves aside and allow the abuse no matter what guilt you might feel. As a mother; I understand that you don't want to devastate your children but by staying you're making it worse for them. They are suffering right aside of you while watching the abuse. You may think that you're hiding it from them but they are more aware than you realize. By using the children as the reason to stay, you are choosing to disrupt their lives by allowing them to witness the daily abuse and tragedy within your home.

I also want you to know that you are not guilty and it is not your fault. There are a lot of people out there who do not understand your situation and may say things to make you feel guilt. You have to remember that they really have no idea what it is like to be in your shoes. I have had people say to me "why didn't you leave sooner?" and I grew tired of trying to make them understand. They also said to me "It's your own fault for staying" like I somehow chose that life. Don't let the ignorance of others deter you from empowering yourself. As I said before, you may lose a lot of friends once you have left the abuse. He may convince them to be on his side, or coerce them much like he did to you and in that case, it is better that they go. You owe nothing to anyone! If they can't see the truth and continually badger you with their questions then it is time to separate yourself.

It is now your time to heal. Your most important first step to that process is to remove any and all negative people from your circle. I can't convince you that this will be easy; I lost a friend of whom I considered one of my closest friends as well as a family member. I can however tell you that you'll feel so much better once all of that toxic negativity is removed from your life. This will leave room for positive people to now enter who can be real support systems.

Try not to dwell on any negative thoughts and I know this will be hard. The guilt that I had within was overwhelming but I had to find a way to overcome it. The first step is understanding that it really is not your fault. Under no circumstances does anyone ever ask to be treated poorly. It is not okay for them to insult you in any way. You did nothing to deserve any name-calling or other demeaning statements. There is no justification for this sort of treatment; there are no excuses for this sort of behavior and you deserve better. Don't ever be made to feel like that sort of behavior is acceptable because it isn't.

You cannot blame yourself for someone else's actions; the problem isn't you it is them.

If they tell you that you have to change because you are the problem, then take a step back and think about that. We have the right to be who we are and shouldn't have to change for anybody. You can be loved for being you and they should love you as you come. If they can't accept you as you are then you need to realize that they probably never will. It's a real lonely existence to be in a relationship where you aren't loved nor accepted for the real you.

A real loving relationship is met halfway. He will care about you and what is important to you and never for a moment expect you to change who you are. You have the right to have friendships and the freedom to enjoy your friends. Do not ever think it is all right to give something up because your partner wants you to. It's your life and only you have the right to choose what is best for you.

When I allowed him to have that power over me, I also allowed him to control my life and that is not okay. We need other people in our lives and the comfort in knowing that we can have ongoing relationships with them. It's healthy to have the ability to drive over and visit someone if we want to. It's human to have the choice to walk out that door and go wherever our hearts lead us without someone trying to tell us otherwise. A person who really loves you would support your decisions and stand by you. They wouldn't lock up that door and dissuade you from anything that you want to do. How are we to succeed in life if we are constantly met with anger and fighting; it is not okay for anyone to discourage you from anything.

The hardest part of your journey is going to be accepting things for yourself. I was you for 21 years; I know what it is like when someone tries to tell you what to do. You either wrestle with shame or guilt and of course the belief that you can make him love you. After the first 5 years of my situation, I realized the hard way that despite my efforts, he didn't love me. He tore apart everything I did to the point of annihilating it. I could do nothing right by his eyes and that continued until the very end. In his eyes I was a whore, a mistake, a cunt, useless, pathetic, too fat, not good enough, too stupid, and clueless. The insults came daily and sometimes with violence attached to them. No matter how hard I worked at being good enough, he just wouldn't ever see it. The only positive that came out of my situation was being fed up with my intelligence being insulted. I worked hard at studying everything from psychology to the techniques of college-level literature. My inner confidence would grow each time I recognized that I was attaining the knowledge from the material I studied. This would only prove to me that I am none of the things he wanted me to believe about myself.

You can do the same thing; but you have to first choose to show yourself that you are worth it. You can do this in many ways that will work for you. Prove to yourself your own worth, whether it is through education or something that you believe you couldn't before do. By at least trying, you prove to yourself that anything can be accomplished no matter how big or small. Make new friends or reach out to the ones you trust. Build up your self-worth so that you can believe that you are anything but what he's tried to convince you of. Once you do empower yourself, nothing will stop you. Not even him.

I want to leave you with this: there will come a day when you will wake up and pull off those blinders. The reality of being contained in a prison-like situation is going to crash down hard upon you but you have to remember to stand back up. Absorb the pain and learn from it. Getting out of it really isn't as hard as we perceive it to be. There is no doubt that he will threaten you, or already has by making statements much like I heard "If you leave me, I will kill you and whoever is around you." That is how they get into your head; similar techniques are used on children after being raped or abused. He may say it a hundred times throughout the course of your relationship much like mine had but know there's help out there. Go file for a stay-away order and hold nothing back. Do not be afraid to confess to the conditions that he had forced you to live in. No judge is going to turn his back to you once you have confessed. Be persistent, and be thorough. It will be uncomfortable and maybe even feel like your heart is about to beat out of your chest but know that the reward is greater.

Seek out help in your road to recovery; there is no shame in visiting with a psychiatrist and going through counseling. Some of you may be like me and could be suffering from Complex-Post Traumatic Stress Disorder and depression. Nobody walks out of an abusive relationship flawless; you are going to be scarred somehow and that is okay. Be thankful that you did finally get out and take the time to work on you.

There is no magic wand to erase your past. Those memories will be with you for a while and it will take you some time to recover but don't let that set you back. Just like we heal from a major surgery, we need the time to fully recover from the mental, emotional and physical abuse that we survived. There are many networks out there that you can reach out to who can help you; Victims of Violence in my area offers free counseling and there are also hotlines in which you can call for assistance. I have even crossed support groups in social-media as well as through blogs and websites across the internet. Do not be afraid to utilize these services, they can help you along your road to recovery.

In time, you will find the right person who will love you and cherish you in the way that you deserve. Do not let your past shadow your future. Keep your guard up, but do not become so defensive that you let nobody in. Believe it or not; most people are not like the abuser and some can't even fathom why anyone would treat another the way that the abuser had. I am sure he did a very good job at convincing you that nobody would want you or even like you but I can tell you from experience that he was just trying to keep you chained down. You have to tell yourself "who is he to speak that over me?" and repeat that as often as possible.

I once asked my abuser why he stuck with me if nobody could love me or want me and before I suffered the repercussions of that, he was quite stumped. He had no idea how to reply and of course I received the name-calling just before he left the house. Every time I questioned him, I was called stupid or ignorant and that's simply because he didn't want to be revealed. All he wanted was something he could control like an object so he could parade it around like his trophy. By questioning anything, I was taking away his control over me and that scared him to death.

My prison sentence began and ended in Chittenango - a place that will always mean something more to me than just a small village in upstate New York. I went into his hell optimistic and full of aspiring dreams. For a long time, I had lost sight of them but that single monarch still fluttered by. I left with those dreams restored and a lot of scars but at least I can say that I walked through hell down a yellow brick road and lived to tell about it.

As the saying goes "where all your hopes and dreams just might come true!"

Never give up.

Chapter 12

"We are looking for a way to feel more real, but we do not realize that to feel more real we have to push ourselves further into the unknown."

~ Mark Epstein

I will now leave you with a poem and an oceanic revelation;

Confession of a Clairvoyant: from Satan to soul mate.

I

O' the world I come to know,

was violent as violent seems,

filled with sorrow and sadly so,

so sadly went mine dreams,
lost in flats of swamp and soot,
aside the bloodied streams -

Smearing fate with pretenses,
an ache that sorely dost grow,
weeping smiles between fences,
submerged in a makeshift gaol,
held mine breastplate to the blade,
in hopes of freeing mine soul.

The hours and days become years,
desolation manifests phantom friends,
wading through the thick of jeers,
first ones render at least tens,
a dash of quietus hast came to be,
from flesh I dare not cleanse.

"O' Teufel, lieber Teufel!"
such pleads 'neath a moon's night,
pressed mine back 'gainst the ground,
a beggar perhaps, desperate I might,
none such came, and none such since,
tho' accursed, whence blest in smite.

But he came as oft as cancer,
permeating sun to ground,

140

in a scream thee wouldst answer,

depleting ration of sound,

and so I spent the daylight after,

headfirst within a cloud.

"To us!" it spits in such malodor,

crowning false such claims,

upon a filthy commode it sits,

reciting to the dames,

such humility hast become of his,

to whom the fool names.

A claimant to lost innocence,

to haste of feeble greed,

suspect of great dissidence,

whose head they must feed,

all was left was but a mote,

the rest was gone to he.

'Neath the nearly twenty since,

of scars and sorrowed sea,

wept the fragile innocent,

upon a weathered lea,

the fire consumed long enough,

until there came a key.

II

"Awake!" scream'd a thunderous voice,
accompanied with the buzz, buzz of AM fuzz:
"Hey-ho Jennuh, ride across the wind,
go-go Jennuh, go on let him in,
no-no Jennuh, what did you begin?
go now Jennuh, go to him within."

From mine hair I shook the dream,
and from mine ears the buzzing buzz,
there I sat among the beam
of a premonition yet to come,
of it weren't what it seemed,
but I deemed it cumbersome -

Then before me rose the screen,
on either side erected pews,
walls outstretched in art decor,
objects hissed by to fuse,
and downward counted 10 to 1,
hastily followed by thicks of queues.

Stranger looking back at me,
out there upon a hill,
surrounded by a great valley,
filled with roses and a rill,

he looked just as sad and lost,
that stranger staring still.

Beside him stood a reverie,
built of chance and sacrifices,
in his eyes I surely see,
the key to end all vices,
but here I sat in company
of empty paradises.

He, the native of stranger land,
became mine rite of Spring,
out there somewhere he lonely stand,
within the hill of many a thing,
but half of me is within 'is eyes,
that half is one will sing.

The raven haired entity
is waiting on the shore,
I must confess I do not know
where or when for sure,
but I know I will get there,
that I'm truly sure.

For now I wait with hopeful eyes,
a heart of much persistence,
this I cannot let get by,

my soul's hungry insistence,

for he is my other side,

and key to completeness.

Oceanic revelations -

At the edge of our well comforted existence we are challenged to push through the invisible boundaries that before confined us within a deceiving warmth. Once comes a day where you just take the leap into the bottomless pit of darkness without knowing where you'll land (if at all.) The cold races to meet your soul with discontent and unconcern for your well-being and the tears gather gently. A light illuminates a pathway filled with jagged rocks and blips of unknown silhouettes in the distance. A surreal sense of euphoria overcomes the momentum of shock and yet ... a small step forward begins. Giant heaps of pain crawl up into your neurons while the tearing lesions spoils the flesh with stains of crimson networking through the tiny grooves. A sudden bolt to the thorax with the ambitions of angina pectoris coupled with dyspnea and presyncope. *Breathe* -

Homeostasis is no longer. Uneven thoughts resulting from a lack of sentient pronounce themselves in sheets of dubiety. You may ask yourself; "where are the people I trust?" A very defined fabrication passes familiar lips to familiar smiles who are beholden to some a cynical of familiar faces.

Some colloquy concerning you turns to a hundred knives impaling you in the posterior region. Isn't it amazing, their little circles? What is trust, if not a sense of loyalty resides in the possession of they who promised you could. The silent road of silhouettes appears as forsaken as you feel within. That of which you used to know is no longer but a substance of scintilla swept away at profound distances - so far, in fact, that the memories wane with the fading sun. Forget what you thought you knew; yesteryear is a greatest distance never again to be experienced, and yet, you coexist with a believable assumption that is as equivocal as the fables of a flawed fabulist.

Finally, fair traveler ... you come to conceive that you are utterly, and entirely forlorn. A revelation of the 'who' and 'how' fills the glass of emptied hope and offers you a new opportunity. Thenceforth ascends a choice; a step back to a false equilibrium, or a step forth to a daunting unknown. (I was you, I commenced forth.)

If by fear you choose the latter; then we must conclude that you chose a fictitious assumption of a temporary comfort that is due to crumble in downward motions which will entomb you prematurely.

If by faith you chose to press forth; fear no longer controls your destiny and although new challenges will emerge, you made a decision to try. For that alone, you have achieved a level of success that most won't ever reach.

Press forth in fearless travels.